BRILLIANT TEAMS

BRILLIANT TEAMS

THE ART AND SCIENCE OF EXCEPTIONAL TEAMS

EMMA CLAYTON

authors
AND CO.

First published in Great Britain in 2024
by Authors & Co.
www.authorsandco.pub

Copyright © Emma Clayton 2024
www.bebrilliant.org.uk

Emma Clayton asserts the moral right to be identified as the author of this work in accordance with the Copyright, Designs and Patents Act 1988.

ISBN 978-1-915771-70-4 (paperback)
ISBN 978-1-915771-79-7 (hardback)

First edition, 2024

This book is lovingly dedicated to two remarkable individuals who have profoundly shaped the person I am today.

To my dad, a beacon of ambition and determination, whose teachings have been the cornerstone of my career. He instilled in me the belief that with hard work and resilience, nothing is beyond our reach. Though we lost him in March 2022, his entrepreneurial spirit and approach to life – "Just be happy" – continue to inspire me daily. He taught me that true success comes not just from what we achieve for ourselves but from the obstacles we overcome along the way and the person we become as a result.

And to my daughter, Molly. Over the last fifteen years, you have been my greatest teacher. Navigating the world as a solo parent, you have taught me the invaluable skills of patience, effective communication, trust and the power of listening. There is no role more rewarding than being your mum, and it's a journey that has positively transformed me in ways I could never have imagined.

Together, you and Grandad have been my guiding stars, teaching me to balance my drive for success with the nurture and humanity of being a mother. Your influence has made me a more compassionate human being, a better mum, an empathic leader and, above all, a woman who is continually learning and growing.

This book is a tribute to the indelible impact you have both had on my life.

May we all thrive as we learn the balance of achievement and humanity, ambition and compassion.

CONTENTS

ABOUT THE AUTHOR

Emma Clayton's award-winning career is a testament to her exceptional ability to guide organisations with strategic insight and a deep understanding of human behaviour. She is the founder of Be Brilliant Consultancy, where her mission is to achieve unprecedented revenue growth for her clients whilst illuminating brilliance within their marketing and executive teams. Emma's strategic marketing and leadership background positions her as a catalyst for change, growth and the kind of impact that transforms the essence of how teams and leaders excel.

As a Marketing Leadership Specialist, sometimes referred to as the 'Mary Poppins for Marketing Teams', Emma empowers marketing departments to reach their fullest potential. Her approach transcends conventional business strategies, focusing on the intricacies of human connections and the power of understanding people.

Emma holds several Non-Executive Director (NED) and part-time Chief Marketing Officer (CMO) roles as well as leading her consultancy business. Her expertise shines in her ability to connect organisations with customers, forge harmonious team environments, and lead transformative growth.

Her work is deeply informed by her academic achievements, including a Chartered Institute of Marketing Fellowship, and two further Postgraduate Diplomas in Organisational Psychology from the University of Aberdeen and Leadership Communications from The University of Cambridge. Emma's commitment to leadership development is profound, advocating for resilience, compassion, and developing full leadership potential.

Emma's influence extends across diverse sectors, including the NHS, life sciences, SaaS and tech scale-ups, showcasing her versatile and impactful abilities. Her certifications as a DiSC behavioural model practitioner and facilitator for Patrick Lencioni's 'Five Dysfunctions of a Team' emphasise her dedication to optimising team dynamics and leadership effectiveness.

A staunch advocate for gender equality in leadership, Emma's contributions to the 2022 All-Party Parliamentary Group (APPG) report for Women in Work highlight her commitment to creating more inclusive workplaces and advancing the dialogue on gender parity.

Emma Clayton is more than a consultant; she is a visionary leader whose holistic approach, combined with her commitment to personal and professional development, positions her as a pivotal figure in driving organisational success, whilst advancing inclusive leadership cultures.

INTRODUCTION

Henry Ford once said, *'Coming together is a beginning, keeping together is progress, working together is success.'* In our rapidly evolving world, this sentiment has never been more pertinent. As we stand on the brink of monumental shifts driven by technological advancements, economic upheavals and the entrance of future generations into the workforce, the essence of how we work together is transforming.

The challenges before us — climate change, war, economic and energy crises and human security — are not only growing in complexity but also in their demand for innovative solutions. These are not puzzles that can be solved in isolation but require the collective brilliance of diverse minds and the gentle touch of human kindness.

Amid the whirlwind of the twenty-first-century digital revolution and the relentless march of AI and technology, I maintain an unwavering belief in the power of relationships to guide those solutions. I believe that the answers to navigating the immense cultural shifts we face will not emerge from the cold logic of machines or the impersonal algorithms of artificial intelligence. Instead, they will spring from the depth of our minds, the warmth of our hearts and the collective, collaborative efforts of our communities.

We often hear 'the whole is greater than the sum of the parts'. This simple truth emphasises the importance of human connection. We are a world made up of beings that are driven by emotions and influenced by the relationships around us. Our human desire to connect with others who share our values and emotions plays a crucial role in tackling the world's most complex challenges. Over time, humans have evolved to work together, and that strategy has continued to succeed much better than any that includes working in isolation.

Without teamwork and communities, our ancient ancestors couldn't have built shelters, hunted game, cultivated land or defended against attacks from other tribes or wild animals. The principle that drove early humans to band together for survival now propels modern societies toward advancement and prosperity, illustrating that the foundation of human progress is, and always has been, our ability to work together effectively. We have an innate reliance on others for our survival.

At the heart of existence, life thrives on collaboration, belonging and mutual support. The notion of going it alone, isolating oneself from the world, isn't just impractical; it's contrary to our very nature. Even those who choose a path of solitude, at some point, depend on others for essentials like food, supplies, or healthcare. The old adage, *'No man (or woman) is an island,'* holds more weight today than ever before in our intricately connected society. To survive and flourish, we depend on the strength, wisdom and companionship of others – building and nurturing relationships in all facets of life.

Despite technological and digital advancements designed to connect us, there's an ironic twist: we're becoming more isolated. In the face of this growing separation, the need to invest in our togetherness – our people, teams and communities – has never been more pressing. Now is the moment to cultivate cultures that champion positive change, empowering and enabling our workforce to achieve shared triumphs and innovations. Those who can master this successfully will not only survive; they'll create communities that thrive and establish new benchmarks of excellence in their domains.

For this reason, workplace teams have become a hot topic. The post-pandemic landscape's shift towards remote and hybrid working models has highlighted the vital need for enhanced collaboration and connectivity within teams. As we strive to adapt our working practices to better accommodate the modern workforce's demands for work-life balance, we've inadvertently stumbled upon a series of new challenges.

Today's leaders find themselves navigating through a maze of complexities, including eroding trust and engagement within teams, elevated stress levels and the challenges of managing a multigenerational workforce. Additionally, they're contending with the aftermath of COVID-19, which brings phenomena like quiet quitting, dwindling morale, retention issues and burnout, as well as the logistical difficulties of overseeing teams scattered across various locations. These are formidable obstacles that demand innovative leadership approaches in this new era.

There is no escaping the fact that today's leaders face intricate and complex challenges. Research indicates that about one third of team members are not fully engaged, with half of this disengaged group considering leaving their organisation. Influenced by phenomena like quiet quitting, a worrying 15% display behaviours that can be detrimental to team cohesion[1]. In this environment, leaders find themselves under immense pressure, recognising their pivotal role in fostering team engagement and driving performance.

---

1. State of the Global Workplace report, Gallup. 2022

We stand at the threshold of a new era in leadership, one that demands a profound understanding of the nuanced human elements of team management. However, a notable omission exists in current leadership development frameworks – a comprehensive strategy to prepare leaders for the intricate challenges that lie ahead remains strikingly absent.

In the pursuit of peak performance, leadership discussions often circle around performance goals such as targets, strategies, outcomes, accountability and engagement – deemed as the holy grail of success – Yet a vital element regularly goes unaddressed: the inherent human need for connection, belonging, and resilience. This lack of understanding, or at worst, neglect, is contributing to a widespread disengagement crisis, and it's significantly affecting overall performance.

The truth is, before we can expect to see sustainable, healthy, long-term results, we need to address the culture within our teams and organisations. Engaging the human element –ensuring team members feel connected, valued, and resilient – is not just a nice-to-have; it's essential. Without a team that's engaged at a fundamental level, achieving lasting results is an uphill battle.

Leaders must shift their focus and strategies to nurture these core psychological needs, thereby laying the groundwork for true high performance. Their role is to develop the team and build and maintain performance whilst creating a level of connectivity that enables the team to thrive and engage in their work collectively.

These teams don't just magically develop overnight. Whilst we live in a world of instant gratification and a desire for a quick-fix magic potion, building a brilliant team takes time and consistency. They're built through deliberate actions, consistent effort and a conducive environment that fosters growth, collaboration and innovation. It takes significant effort for a leader to instil a sense of productivity, performance and culture needed to produce exceptional results.

Can you recall when you were last part of a highly productive, dynamic and inspirational team? I'm sure it was an uplifting experience, characterised by a sense of unity, purpose and momentum. The camaraderie, mutual respect and shared enthusiasm for the task at hand not only propelled your team towards its goals but also fostered an environment where you felt valued, motivated and engaged. This collective energy and drive no doubt made challenges more surmountable and successes more rewarding, creating memorable moments that you still cherish.

Conversely, the experience of being part of a less harmonious, dysfunctional team often leads to feelings of disheartenment. Characterised by frustration, disconnection and stagnation, such teams struggle with trust issues, poor communication and ambiguous goals, fostering an environment ripe for misunderstandings and diminished productivity. This lack of harmony and clear direction can result in feeling undervalued and disengaged, exacerbating tensions and conflicts. The resultant silo mentality and self-preservation over collaborative effort not only undermine the team's effectiveness but also takes a toll on individual well-being, leaving members feeling exhausted and discontented.

And the impact doesn't end there. The repercussions of dysfunctional teams extend further, affecting the customer experience significantly. Poor morale among team members dampens their drive to provide exceptional service. Poor communication hampers internal efficiency and significantly degrades the customer experience through incongruency and inconsistencies. These teams, plagued by a lack of effective collaboration, frequently face decision-making and problem-solving delays, which in turn cause extended response times to customer inquiries.

This lack of enthusiasm and engagement hinders the team's ability to innovate and adapt to customers' evolving needs, leading to a decline in service quality. The inevitable fallout? A damaged brand reputation, as dissatisfied customers don't hesitate to seek alternatives and share their negative experiences. In today's market, where consumers are more informed and demanding than ever, the importance of honing our teams to meet these high expectations cannot be overstated. Success in consistently satisfying customer expectations is crucial for the long-term prosperity of any business.

Despite best efforts, many organisations need help. They are trapped in feast or famine revenue generation patterns, siloed thinking and decreasing engagement. This book is written to help break that cycle. It can guide you to build collaborative, resilient and high-performing teams, ready to tackle today's and tomorrow's challenges and surpass your customer's expectations.

BEYOND HIGH PERFORMANCE: EMBRACING THE SHIFT TO BRILLIANCE

The phrase 'high performance' is widely used throughout organisations and in popular literature, yet it is hardly ever clearly defined. The criteria typically include a sentiment around 'constantly achieving or exceeding targets', 'agile and resilient to shifting priorities', 'score highly on an employee survey', or 'has a reputation where people want to be part of it'. Clear as mud, right?

I think it is time to reconsider this overused term 'high-performing teams'. Simply labelling a team or organisation as 'high-performing' no longer captures what today's workforce needs. The term overlooks the essence of what distinguishes a truly remarkable team – and it's more than just performance!

By dictionary definitions, the word 'brilliant' shines back at us with meanings like 'very bright and radiant' and 'exceptionally clever or talented'. Being 'brilliant' encompasses not just achieving excellent results, formulating competitive strategies, fostering innovation and reaching goals; it's also about cultivating a profound sense of unity and mutual understanding among team members. Brilliance in a team context includes the culture we build, our empathy, how we communicate and listen and our resilience in the face of setbacks. It involves integrating emotional intelligence and a human touch into our collective successes. So, in its simplest terms, being a **brilliant** team means we're good at what we do, and we are good to each other.

We must embrace this fuller meaning of brilliance. A team that lights up not just because of its achievements but HOW it achieves them – together, with warmth and a shared sense of humanity – is the kind of brilliance we should all aspire to, and it's what teams crave.

Brilliant teams are not just a collection of skills and knowledge but dynamic entities that adapt, evolve and thrive through challenges. They create spaces where individuals feel valued, heard and empowered to contribute their best, making the collective sum far greater than its individual parts. In this light, the brilliance of a team is not merely a measure of performance or capability but a testament to the environment that shapes, supports and elevates it to new heights. High performance, in its traditional sense, is outdated and, I would argue, possibly even obsolete; it's the cultivation of an environment and culture prioritising continuous learning collaboration, and innovation that truly drives results beyond just metrics.

MASTERING THE ART AND SCIENCE OF TEAMWORK

Mastering teamwork and leadership is both an art and a science. It requires emotional intelligence to navigate interpersonal dynamics and strategic thinking to align diverse talents towards a common objective. It's about knowing when to lead, when to follow, when to push for your idea and when to back someone else's.

The good news is that these skills can be learned. This book is your playbook, providing the essentials of effective teamwork, practical advice and steps to build that brilliant team. Whether stepping into your first leadership role or just looking to improve your collaboration, you'll find strategies and insights that you can apply in any team setting.

Are you facing team retention challenges, striving for stronger trust and collaboration, or navigating constant change? This book provides a comprehensive guide to graceful conflict resolution, enhancing team emotional intelligence and achieving a balance that encourages performance without risking burnout. You'll discover how to align individual strengths with team objectives, ensuring peak performance. This book equips you with strategies for fostering resilience and innovation, enabling your team to excel in adversity, pursue continuous improvement and gain practical leadership skills to instantly boost team engagement and performance.

Designed for a wide audience, from team leaders and members aiming for higher productivity and innovation, to those seeking practical strategies for building exceptional teams, this book is a resource for project leaders, organisational heads, entrepreneurs, HR professionals, communication specialists and learning and development experts. It offers transformative insights for anyone interested in enhancing workplace dynamics, promising to reshape your view and achieve outstanding results, irrespective of your role.

Why did I write this book?

My career began in marketing, where I cultivated a passion for deepening customer connections and fostering brand loyalty. However, I soon realised that the most brilliant strategies and plans were rendered ineffective without cohesive team communication and collaboration. A strategy's success hinges on its execution excellence, which steered me towards a deeper exploration of team behaviour and leadership dynamics, and a greater understanding of why my strategies weren't effectively implemented.

I delved into team psychology and behavioural science, recognising its critical importance for achieving marketing success. The common challenges of team misalignment and ineffective communication I encountered highlighted the urgent need to prioritise team performance and culture when aiming for high performance; 'soft skills' were actually the most critical skills.

This book was born out of a desire to offer a single, comprehensive guide for constructing exceptional teams. It is the culmination of that exploration, aimed at equipping leaders with the necessary tools and insights to navigate the complexities of the modern workplace and inspire meaningful change in organisational success.

What This Book Doesn't Cover

I've chosen not to explore a few big topics in this book: Executive Presence, Thought Leadership, Team Capability and Skills, Multigenerational and Remote teams, and Personality Types. It's not because they aren't important – they really are! But plenty of other books out there already cover these topics in depth.

In crafting this book, I wanted to offer you something distinct, a blend of insights you won't find elsewhere. My focus? Illuminating the core elements that empower teams to excel and achieve remarkable outcomes together. While my work with clients and leaders often involves enhancing leadership styles, establishing thought leadership and boosting team capabilities, this book zooms in on the secret sauce that transforms a team from good to brilliant. You can find resources about the other subjects in the resource section at the back of the book.

The decision to bypass other important topics was intentional, aiming to concentrate on actionable strategies that metamorphose a collection of individuals into a formidable force. This is about enriching your leadership toolkit with fresh, impactful approaches. That's my mission here.

HOW TO READ THIS BOOK

This book is structured in three sections.

Section One delves into the essence of brilliant teams, distinguishing between leadership and management roles and examining how team dynamics have evolved. It introduces a crucial framework, blending the science of performance enhancement with the art of nurturing a positive team culture. This segment provides a foundational understanding of what differentiates a functional team from a truly exceptional one, highlighting the importance of both evidence-based strategies and empathetic leadership in adapting to modern workplace challenges. Through this exploration, readers will uncover the keys to building and leading teams that are not only high-performing but also innovative and resilient.

Section Two, 'THE SCIENCE OF A BRILLIANT TEAM', delves into the performance metrics and frameworks that underpin team effectiveness. It offers a deep dive into the organisational principles that govern team dynamics, providing the scientific insights and processes necessary to assess and enhance team performance systematically. This section equips you with the knowledge to measure, analyse and optimise the workings of your team, grounded in evidence-based practices.

Section Three, 'THE ART OF A BRILLIANT TEAM', focuses on the cultural aspects vital for leading a brilliant team. It emphasises the importance of nurturing a conducive team environment that fosters collaboration, innovation and resilience. This section guides you through the nuances of creating a culture where brilliant teams can thrive, highlighting leadership and team behaviours, communication strategies, and team-building practices that cultivate a strong, unified and adaptable team ethos.

Each section of this book is a critical piece of the puzzle in understanding and cultivating brilliance within teams. By integrating the insights from all three, you are empowered to lead with both the art and science of brilliant team management, ensuring your team not only excels in its achievements but does so in a manner that is sustainable, fulfilling and aligned with the evolving landscape of work.

While each chapter is penned to stand alone, allowing you to delve into specific topics as needed, the fullest and most enriching experience comes from reading the book in its entirety. This approach ensures a comprehensive grasp of how the individual facets of team brilliance interconnect and reinforce one another. Ready to begin?

SECTION I

THE ANATOMY OF A BRILLIANT TEAM

'Being a leader has a lot to do with helping other people achieve what they can achieve.'

— CHRISTINE LAGARDE

The importance of having a brilliant team in today's business landscape cannot be overstated; it's a hot topic (and challenge) among many leaders. A brilliant team, which may sound idealistic to some, is essentially a cohesive unit where every member leverages their unique skills towards a shared objective, actively engages in decision-making and embraces successes and failures as collective experiences. Such teams should not be a fantasy but become a practical reality where effective communication and a robust sense of unity underpin organisational success.

These dynamic groups resemble superheroes of the corporate world, thriving on efficiency and satisfaction. They break free from the confines of traditional nine-to-five roles to take charge of their work lives through curiosity, adaptability, growth mindsets and proactive collaboration. This shift signals a move from outdated hierarchical management, as today's employees demand meaningful involvement in the decisions and operations of the business. Leaders and managers are challenged to evolve, fostering an environment where open communication and teamwork are paramount, emphasising that a united team is exponentially more powerful than the sum of its individual members.

LEADERSHIP, MANAGEMENT AND TEAMS

Leaders need to learn how to build brilliant teams. Often elevated to their positions for their technical expertise and mastery in their field (e.g., accounting, law or science), they face a pivotal challenge as they ascend the career ladder. They soon discover that the very skills that propelled them to leadership roles – deep technical knowledge and cognitive abilities – are not the tools to ensure their success as leaders.

Transitioning from an outstanding technician to an effective leader requires a fundamental shift in competencies and behaviours. Newly appointed leaders find themselves navigating the complex dynamics of diverse teams, where strategic leadership, team engagement and a move from focusing on operations to embracing strategy become essential. This realisation marks a crucial point in their professional journey, as they must learn and adopt new ways of leading to build and sustain brilliant teams. As individuals transition from team leader to manager, manager to leader and leader to senior leader, a diverse set of behaviours becomes essential, especially in areas such as strategy, engagement and the skill of uniting a team.

Consider leadership as the individual who establishes the atmosphere, the visionary who motivates others. The focus is on the team's and company's reasons and objectives. Leaders act as motivators, consistently encouraging you to perform at your highest level. Imagine having a leader who recognises your strengths and motivates you to excel – it can truly make a difference.

The most successful leaders adeptly balance working 'in' the business with working 'on' it, striving to add value through strategic vision rather than remaining purely operational. They prioritise their teams above themselves, understanding that a team's strength – characterised by a robust blend of performance and culture – is key to propelling the organisation forward. Such leaders create teams that become the engine of organisational success.

While the terms 'leadership' and 'management' are often used interchangeably, they embody distinct yet complementary roles. Leadership is about setting direction and inspiring people to follow. In contrast, management focuses on executing plans and overseeing the day-to-day operations. Both are crucial for the success of any team or organisation.

Management focuses more on day-to-day operations to ensure smooth functioning. Management is a set of well-known processes, like planning, budgeting, structuring jobs, staffing jobs, measuring performance and problem-solving, which help an organisation do what it knows to do well predictably. Management helps you produce products and services as you have promised, of consistent quality and on budget, day after day, week after week. This is an enormously difficult task in organisations of any size and complexity, with complexities often underestimated.

Leadership is entirely different. It is associated with taking an organisation into the future, finding opportunities and successfully exploiting them. Leadership is about vision, motivating people to buy into that vision, empowerment and, most of all, producing useful change. Leadership is not about attributes; it's about behaviour. And in an ever-faster-moving world, leadership is increasingly needed from more and more of us, no matter where you are in a hierarchy. The notion that a few extraordinary people at the top can provide all the leadership needed today is ridiculous and a recipe for failure.

Over the years, the critical role of teams in organisational success has become increasingly clear, elevating the expectation for leaders to not only work effectively within teams but also to amplify their performance. Leadership excellence is often gauged by one's ability to manage and uplift a team.

Brilliant teams foster innovation and ensure adaptability, which is essential in fast-evolving sectors like technology and science. They excel in problem-solving and can quickly pivot in response to new challenges. Research has shown that high-performing teams significantly enhance employee satisfaction, engagement and loyalty[1]. Additionally, organisations that cultivate exceptional teams often lead their markets, experience swift growth, operate efficiently and distinguish themselves within their industries.

EVOLUTION OF LEADERSHIP

Team dynamics have transformed over time. Previously, workplaces were marked by rigid hierarchies and a clear chain of command, under the belief that the hierarchical structure enhanced efficiency. But these sentiments have evolved over time – factors like globalisation, technological advancements and a diverse workforce influence today's team landscape. Globalisation has broadened teams, bringing together individuals from different regions and necessitating cutting-edge technology for seamless connectivity.

As technology advances and globalisation continues, the importance of teams is set to increase even further. The advancement of AI and discussions around sustainability introduce richer challenges.

---

1. Harvard Business Reviews. March 2022. 'How-employee-experience-impacts-your-bottom-line'

What is the solution? Great leadership. In today's professional environment, leaders must adapt to challenges, demonstrate resilience, promote teamwork and adaptability and be willing to delegate responsibilities to team members. This is a completely different world than before, and successful organisations accept change, take the lead and set the standard for others.

Researchers estimate that 14% to 45% of an organisation's financial results derive from executive leadership[2]. Leaders do not achieve these results single-handedly but create conditions that impact team effectiveness.

In fact, the rate of incompetent management is estimated to be 50% to 75%, meaning most managers aren't effective leaders[3]. Regardless of their management status, effective leaders are defined by their ability to build and lead a brilliant team – bad leadership can cost us our wellbeing.

Most of us have had incompetent, hostile or absentee leaders in the workplace who have caused us great misery. 65% of people say the most stressful part of life is their immediate boss[4]. Successful leaders provide an environment that positively supports employees' ability to contribute to organisational goals. In today's dynamic work environment, the influence of a leader on their team is more critical than ever, with the outcomes and longevity of employment increasingly hinging on the quality of leadership.

Unlike past generations, who might have tolerated less-than-ideal leadership due to a sense of loyalty or lack of options, modern

2. Hogan, R., Raskin, R., & Fazzini, D. (1990). The Dark Side of Charisma. In K. E. Clark & M. B. Clark (Eds.), Measures of Leadership (pp. 343–354). Leadership Library of America.

3. Hogan, R. 1994. Trouble at the Top: Causes and Consequences of Managerial Incompetence. Consulting Psychology Journal: Practice and Research, 46(1), 9–15. https://doi.org/10.1037/1061-4087.46.1.9

4. Kaiser, R. B., R. Hogan, & S. B. Craig. 2008. Leadership and the Fate of Organizations. American Psychologist, 63(2), 96–110. https://doi.org/10.1037/0003-066X.63.2.96

employees, particularly younger generations, have shown they will not hesitate to leave positions where leadership fails to meet their expectations. This underlines that the tenure and success of the workforce are deeply connected to the capabilities and behaviour of their leaders.

In short, who is in charge matters!

WHY SOME EXISTING TEAM MODELS DON'T HELP LEADERS

Team dynamics have undergone a significant transformation, yet many models used to build and assess teams have not evolved at the same pace. Traditional frameworks like Tuckman's stages of group development, Belbin's Team Roles and the Myers-Briggs Type Indicator, while providing valuable insights into team behaviour and individual preferences, fall short of fully addressing the complex realities of contemporary teams. These models, which have been instrumental in shaping our understanding of team dynamics, now reveal their limitations in a work landscape characterised by rapid change and the need for nuanced human connections and strategic agility.

Today's teams demand an approach that encapsulates not just behavioural insights but also strategic alignment, emotional intelligence and a capacity for adaptation. The shift from rigid hierarchical structures to dynamic, cross-functional teams requires new leadership strategies that embrace strategic clarity, deep engagement and a culture that champions both individual talent and team synergy. Leaders must surpass these traditional paradigms to cultivate teams that are not merely efficient but exemplary – teams that epitomise innovation, unity and resilience.

It's clear that the modern workforce, with its evolving expectations and fluid team dynamics, is profoundly influenced by the quality of its leadership. Team performance outcomes and longevity are increasingly dependent on leaders who can navigate these changes effectively. In an era where a mismatch with leadership can lead to swift exits, adapting to and adopting new models for team development is beneficial and essential for sustaining brilliance in teams.

THE ANATOMY OF A BRILLIANT TEAM

Before exploring new models to enhance team performance, it's vital to grasp the essence of what constitutes a genuinely brilliant team. This understanding serves as a foundational guide for assembling teams that excel in performance and do so in a manner that's both artful and scientific. The anatomy of a brilliant team encompasses more than just the measurable outputs; it delves into the 'how' – the processes and the human elements such as trust, communication and emotional intelligence that underpin success.

Leaders need this holistic perspective to navigate the complex interplay of factors that make a team truly exceptional. It's not just about following a set formula; it's about fostering a culture where both the scientific methodologies and the art of creating strong, cohesive teams are nurtured, allowing for a harmonious blend of productivity and interpersonal harmony.

THE ART AND SCIENCE OF BRILLIANT TEAMS

Creating and leading exceptional teams is an art and a science, a combination of measurable strategies and the human touch. The successful blend and balance of both is the backbone of team success – where science addresses the structured approach to performance and the art delves into interpersonal relationships and soft skills. Understanding this distinction and how they complement each other is crucial for cultivating a space where brilliance blooms and thrives.

THE SCIENCE OF TEAM PERFORMANCE

The science component of a brilliant team is rooted in the tangible, quantifiable aspects of team leadership – setting clear objectives, devising strategic plans and establishing frameworks that guide the team's direction. This is where we talk about goal setting, performance metrics and the methodologies that enable a team to track progress and assess effectiveness. It involves the development of systems and processes that ensure tasks are completed, deadlines are met and outcomes are achieved.

When applying team dynamic science, leaders focus on the 'what' – what needs to be done to meet the vision, what strategies will drive innovation and what changes need to be implemented to navigate challenges. The science of team leadership emphasises structure and logic, relying on data and evidence to make informed decisions. It's about leveraging tools and technologies to enhance efficiency and foster a culture of continuous improvement.

THE ART OF TEAM DYNAMICS

Conversely, the art of leading teams is inherently more subjective. It focuses on the 'how' – how team members interact, communicate and build relationships. This sphere is characterised by emotional intelligence, empathy, adaptability and the ability to inspire and motivate. Softer skills come into play here, skills that are crucial for creating an environment of trust, respect and mutual support.

The art of teamwork is about understanding the unique personalities within the team, recognising each other's strengths and knowing how to blend these diverse talents into a cohesive unit. It requires a keen sense of awareness, not only of yourself but also of others, and the capacity to navigate the complex dynamics of human behaviour. Leadership in this context is not just about directing; it's about connecting, empowering and creating a sense of belonging.

This side of team management emphasises the importance of communication – not merely exchanging information but creating a space where ideas can be freely shared and voices can be heard, fostering a culture where feedback is not just accepted but encouraged, conflicts are resolved constructively and the collective well-being of the team is a priority.

THE INTERPLAY BETWEEN ART AND SCIENCE

The most successful teams master both the art and science of team dynamics. They balance a structured approach to achieving their goals with a fluid, empathetic understanding of individual team members. It's a dance between rigorously applying performance frameworks and intuitively understanding human needs and motivations.

Leaders who excel at creating and leading exceptional teams understand that science provides the roadmap. Still, the art ensures that the journey is meaningful and inclusive. They recognise that frameworks and plans are necessary for clarity and direction, but achieving true brilliance is unattainable without the human element – empathy, communication and emotional intelligence.

As we delve further into the book's main content, we explore the practical steps and strategies (the science) and the softer, more nuanced aspects of team leadership (the art). This combination forms the essence of building and leading high-performing teams that are truly exceptional.

THE BRILLIANT TEAM ASSESSMENT TOOL

Before we dive into the heart of this book, let's take a moment for an essential preliminary step: auditing your team with the Brilliant Team Assessment Tool.

As we embark on this journey together, understanding where your team currently stands will help you identify the specific chapters and insights most relevant to your needs. If time is tight, this tool allows you to selectively navigate through the content, focusing on areas that require the most attention. I recognise how valuable your time is and this step is designed to maximise the benefits you derive from our time together.

I'm excited to introduce the Brilliant Team Assessment Tool, a resource designed to illuminate your team's strengths and areas for development, focusing on the crucial blend of performance and culture. This innovative tool, grounded in my comprehensive framework, helps pinpoint precisely where your team may be shining or lacking in these essential areas.

Surprisingly, 65% of teams struggle with accountability, unclear on how their roles fit into the organisation's larger strategy or how their efforts contribute to overarching objectives[1]. This lack of clarity often means team performance goes unmeasured against any standard. The assessment tool is designed to eliminate this ambiguity, clearly showing where your team stands and offering strategies to forge a truly brilliant team.

The tool is swift and insightful, taking no more than fifteen minutes to complete, yet, it provides immediate results and actionable steps for improvement. Designed with you in mind, the report delves deep into your team's dynamics, offering strategic insights crucial for growth. The assessment comprises sixty in-depth questions, ensuring a comprehensive analysis with absolute transparency and no ambiguity. Responses are gauged on a ten-point scale, allowing for a detailed understanding of team members' perspectives.

The report you receive at the end provides outcomes that can be integrated directly into your leadership KPIs, ensuring that team development aligns with the organisation's broader objectives.

You can find the tool at:
www.bebrilliantaudit.com/brilliantteamassessment

---

1. Harvard Business Review. February 2022. 'Does-your-team-have-an-accountability-problem

THE BRILLIANT TEAMS
FRAMEWORK

BRILLIANT TEAM FRAMEWORK

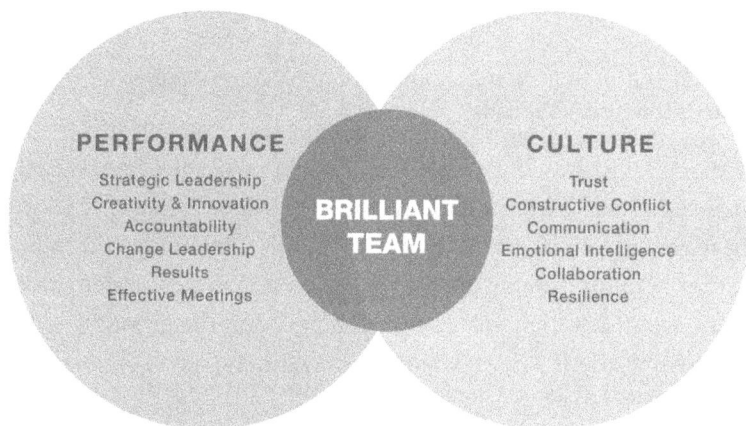

PERFORMANCE

Strategic Leadership
Creativity & Innovation
Accountability
Change Leadership
Results
Effective Meetings

BRILLIANT TEAM

CULTURE

Trust
Constructive Conflict
Communication
Emotional Intelligence
Collaboration
Resilience

PERFORMANCE: THE SCIENCE OF BRILLIANT TEAMS

Understanding the science behind team performance is fundamental for leaders because it provides a framework based on empirical evidence for what works. The science of performance understands what teams need to do to be able to do their best work. It's crucial because it helps us determine the best ways to achieve goals, adapt to changes and generate new ideas.

Strategy

When a team has a clear strategy and knows its direction, it's like having a roadmap for success. This clarity helps everyone understand how to achieve the team's goals, ensuring the whole team works together effectively. A well-defined strategy involves setting, regularly reviewing and communicating the team's priorities. These priorities help meet the organisation's key financial goals and keep everyone focused. When a team has a strong sense of its purpose and direction, it's better at making decisions, understanding each other's priorities and adjusting to new challenges. This makes a big difference in achieving success.

Innovation and Creativity

In today's fast-moving world, innovation is key to keeping any business afloat. With technology zooming ahead, research making big leaps and AI changing how we operate, staying ahead in our market is more difficult than ever. Add to that the unpredictable global scene, a society hungry for the new and the economy's ups and downs, and it's clear: businesses need to be quick on their feet and ready to adapt.

Teams that are ahead of the curve, coming up with fresh, creative ideas are the ones who can handle surprises and tough times better. They're also bringing the most value to their businesses by introducing new and different ways of doing things. When teams dive into various innovative processes and strategies, they contribute to their organisation's ability to innovate and set the stage for beating the competition and boosting overall performance.

But how do you turn those groundbreaking ideas into reality? How do you create an environment where innovation is not only welcomed but part of your organisation's very fabric?

Accountability

Teams with low accountability are common, with some studies showing it affects up to 65% of teams. This is often characterised as a blame-shifting culture where nobody wants to take responsibility. But accountability is something we all need to own, both as individuals and collectively as a team. And that starts with how we behave. When team members feel at ease holding each other accountable in a positive and supportive way, achieving results becomes much more likely. It creates a culture where everyone is responsible for meeting goals, making teams far more successful.

It is essential to create an environment where responsibility and trust go hand in hand and where everyone is open to receiving feedback. Mutual accountability means sticking to what's been agreed upon and taking care of our share of the work, ensuring tasks are assigned and completed properly.

Change Leadership

Dealing with change can be tough, and dealing with constant change can be exhausting! Implementing change can seem impossible. Teams can get knocked off course, lose the teamwork spirit, rebel, lose confidence and become fearful and self-interested. However, embracing the idea that performance can improve through change involves accepting that things might start feeling uncertain. Being good at managing and leading change is essential for a team's peak performance.

Being effective at navigating change and actively looking for chances to leverage change to the team's advantage, both inside and outside the organisation, is a crucial strategy for boosting team efficiency and enhancing organisational results. Embracing a forward-looking attitude and growth mindset enables teams to handle uncertainty better and manage the stress of change.

Results

Suppose that teams don't focus on consistently delivering top-notch results. In that case, there's a high chance they'll be unproductive and not meet their goals. What we focus on is what we achieve. Emphasising results and having a way to monitor progress towards achieving them is crucial for any team strategy. Helping teams pinpoint what success and effectiveness mean in terms of results plays a vital role in grasping their current performance level and what they're capable of achieving in the future.

Meeting Effectiveness

We've all been there, sitting through a meeting and walking out at the end wondering what the point was. In today's corporate world, endless meetings are a common issue, often leading to indecision and little progression. Many of us have seen executives swamped with back-to-back meetings, watching precious time vanish in a blur of inefficiency. Yet, amidst this frustration, there's a glimmer of hope. The answer isn't to scrap meetings altogether but to make them more effective.

As organisations lean more towards consultative and collaborative work styles, there's a certainty that team meetings aren't as productive as they could be. Teams that hold efficient, focused meetings are better positioned to use their time wisely. Since meetings are key for teams to coordinate and collaborate, ensuring they are effective is essential for boosting team engagement and overall performance.

CULTURE: THE ART OF BRILLIANT TEAMS

Team culture is the DNA of the group, comprised of each member's values, the deep-seated reasons and preferences that drive our ambitions and what we're ready to strive for. When these core values clash, team unity is hard to achieve, disagreements can turn personal and people are likely to leave. Culture is built by the everyday behaviour in the workplace that shapes how the team functions. The collective habits and principles guide how team members interact and collaborate to reach their goals. Culture also influences the team's behaviour and value standards, moulding how they work together to fulfil a shared mission. But several elements create that culture.

Trust

Trust is the cornerstone of any team. Without it, teams often find themselves on the defensive, struggling to connect on a level that fosters true unity and collaboration. Trust between team members lays the groundwork for cohesion, creating a safe space where the team can truly unite. Trust isn't a 'nice to have'; it's a critical driver of team performance, underpinning vital outcomes like effective communication and overall satisfaction. Everything is built on trust.

Constructive Conflict

Professional conflict in teams can stem from a basic lack of trust, leading to a hesitancy in open and honest communication. This fear of confronting differences means team members might shy away from discussions that could uncover real intentions or tensions, causing uncertainty about the team's goals and priorities.

Teams that embrace a culture of professional and constructive conflict are more open to expressing concerns and arguments for the team's benefit. This openness helps tackle issues before they become bigger problems, preserving the team's effectiveness and unity. Effectively managed conflict strengthens team cohesion and relationships and boosts team performance, viability and satisfaction.

Communication

How team members talk to each other is crucial in determining the team's performance. Good communication within the team is key as it significantly influences team members' experiences and feelings about being part of the team, especially if teams are in different locations. Open, honest and effective communication helps establish a culture where everyone feels comfortable sharing ideas and feedback. Clear communication is vital to creating a mutual understanding of how the team works, which is essential for achieving top-notch results.

Emotional Intelligence

Emotional Intelligence (EI) has become a key focus in understanding what makes leaders and teams effective. EI is centred around recognising and handling your emotions and those of the people around you. During stressful times, it's easy for people to react based on feelings rather than logic, leading to mistakes. The emotional intelligence of each team member plays a crucial role in how well the team manages emotionally charged situations that are bound to happen.

Interestingly, a team's emotional intelligence affects internal dynamics and enhances customer service quality and overall performance by improving team members' interactions. While understanding and developing EI in a team setting is more complex than on an individual level, teams can grow their collective emotional intelligence, significantly improving their performance.

Collaboration

Collaboration is a game-changer for team performance. Fostering a spirit of teamwork is essential for reaching objectives that one person alone can't tackle. Teams that truly embrace collaboration often establish clear norms and expectations about supporting each other actively and sharing insights and information to secure a win for the whole group. This collaborative mindset isn't just about getting along better; it's a fundamental process that enhances how well a team works together, making coordination smoother and boosting overall team effectiveness.

Resilience

Resilience is key to a team's ability to handle complexity and overcome obstacles successfully. How a team deals with stress and challenges offers vital clues about its culture and ability to sustain high performance over time. Building resilience within a team is crucial as it equips members with the strength and vitality needed to forge strong relationships, adapt to changes and pursue success with determination.

KEY TAKEAWAYS

- **Persistent Challenge of Team Engagement**: Engagement within teams remains a critical issue, directly impacting performance. It's clear that for teams to excel, engagement must be actively fostered and maintained.
- **Evolution of Team Dynamics**: The changing face of team dynamics, influenced by various external and internal factors, requires leaders to adopt innovative leadership styles and strategies that cater to these new dynamics.
- **Redefining Models of Performance and Culture**: Traditional models focusing solely on performance or culture are no longer sufficient. A holistic integration of performance excellence and a strong, positive culture is essential for optimal results.
- **Importance of Brilliant Teams**: Brilliant teams are vital for organisational success, embodying the skills, knowledge and drive needed to navigate complex challenges, foster innovation and achieve standout results.
- **Science and Art of Team Construction**: Building a brilliant team requires a balanced approach; the science involves employing evidence-based practices for strategy, innovation and efficiency, while the art focuses on soft skills such as empathy, trust and resilience.

By embracing the Brilliant Team framework, organisations can forge teams that are equipped to tackle today's challenges and resilient and innovative enough to thrive in the ever-changing business landscape. This approach ensures teams are not just performing tasks but are engaged, motivated and aligned with the broader organisational goals, setting the stage for sustained success and excellence.

SECTION II

THE SCIENCE OF BRILLIANT TEAMS

Team science delves into what propels a team toward collective success. It involves thoroughly examining the essential components that inspire and direct a team to achieve remarkable feats together. In this section, we'll unravel what it takes for teams to excel in unison, setting the stage for extraordinary performance.

How many teams have you been in where you had no idea what the goal or vision of the organisation was? Or where the organisation was heading? Clearly defined strategies, goals and a long-term vision are at the core of any brilliant team. These elements act as the team's compass, guiding every decision and action. A well-articulated strategy provides a clear path forward, allowing team members to navigate their roles with a sense of direction and purpose. Goals serve as their milestones along this path, offering tangible targets that maintain focus and motivation. The vision acts as the beacon of possibility, inspiring innovation and creativity in the team by painting a picture of what the future could hold if the team achieves its goal.

Innovation and creativity create the possibilities for any team striving not just to meet the status quo but to redefine it. In a constantly changing world with increasing customer demands, thinking outside the box, seeing beyond the immediate and imagining new solutions to old problems sets brilliant teams apart. However, creativity isn't just about having ideas; it's also about the team's ability to bring those ideas to life. This requires an environment where team members feel valued and encouraged to share their thoughts and perspectives, knowing that their contributions are an essential part of the team's innovation process, along with the ability to listen actively to customers and respond with solutions to challenges.

In today's fast-paced world, change is the only constant. Brilliant teams not only anticipate change but embrace it as an opportunity for growth and learning. Their ability to pivot, adapt strategies and overcome challenges with resilience allows them to thrive in uncertainty.

Creating results is, ultimately, the most tangible measure of a team's performance – turning vision into reality, ideas into outcomes and challenges into successes. But achieving remarkable results isn't just about hard work; it's about working smart, leveraging each team member's strengths and ensuring that efforts are aligned with the team's overarching goals and strategy. It's here that the importance of meeting effectively comes into play. Team meetings are not merely administrative check-ins or talking shops; they are strategic gatherings where ideas are shared, decisions are made, progress is assessed and collective wisdom is tapped into to overcome obstacles and identify new opportunities.

Playing to strengths is perhaps one of a team's most strategic moves. It acknowledges that brilliance isn't about individual heroics but how well individuals' strengths are woven together to create a fabric of collective competence and innovation. This method empowers team members to excel in their areas of expertise, harnessing their diverse strengths to craft a unified ensemble of brilliance. As we explore the science of a team, we delve into these components not as isolated elements but as interconnected facets of a holistic system.

This section focuses on aligning strategy, innovation, adaptability and results orientation while leveraging the synergistic interplay of strengths. Here, you'll discover invaluable insights and tools to cultivate an environment where these elements not only exist but flourish, propelling your team towards unparalleled success.

By the end of this section, you'll have a deeper appreciation of the foundational elements underpinning team performance and a roadmap for integrating these principles into your team's dynamics.

1

STRATEGIC LEADERSHIP

One day Alice came to a fork in the road and saw a Cheshire cat in a tree. 'Which road do I take?' she asked. 'Where do you want to go?' was his response. 'I don't know,' Alice answered. 'Then,' said the cat, 'it doesn't matter.'

In today's fast-paced business world, a strategy is more than just a plan. A strategy helps you figure out how to move forward as an organisation through market volatility, changing customer needs and competitive challenges, and turn those challenges into opportunities. If your plan is too broad or vague or, in the case of many of the organisations I work with, a list of endless tactics, then it's not really a strategy at all.

In much the same way, an organisation without a clear strategy is akin to Alice without a destination. Without a defined path forward, any road will do, but the result is a directionless journey filled with uncertainty and missed opportunities. Just as Alice needed clarity to navigate Wonderland, organisations require a strategic compass to guide their actions and achieve their goals.

Developing a clear strategy is like planning an exciting journey to an incredible destination. It begins by knowing precisely where we're headed and understanding our starting point. With numerous paths available – some scenic, others quicker – we must navigate wisely. Along the way, we'll make stops for refreshments, fuel and rest, and should we encounter unexpected obstacles (roadworks), having a backup plan is crucial.

A well-crafted strategy serves as our roadmap, guiding us to make informed decisions that propel us closer to our destination. It fosters team cohesion, ensuring everyone remains motivated and aligned, all travelling together on the same route. Imagine arriving at our destination only to discover that half the team didn't make it – an undesirable outcome for any successful journey.

Strategy serves as the cornerstone for steering teams towards success within your organisation. It provides a defined path and a purpose, motivating them to align their efforts with the broader organisational objectives. Without this guiding framework, team members risk aimlessly wandering, unsure of their destination or how to reach it.

Imagine embarking on a journey without a map or clear directions. Teams may soon find themselves lost, encountering obstacles without a clear course of action. Without a strategic direction, efforts can become scattered, resources wasted and team members frustrated with the lack of progress.

I'm certain you've been part of a team tackling a significant project without a clear plan, experiencing the frustration of misalignment and conflict it can breed. Picture your team members pulling in various directions, uncertain of priorities and consistently missing deadlines. Sadly, real-life scenarios like these are all too common – businesses missing out on vital opportunities and projects veering off course due to the absence of a guiding strategy. Even the most skilled teams can falter without that guiding star, underscoring the critical importance of starting with a robust strategy.

At its core, strategy embodies a commitment from our leaders to navigate the uncertainties and select the optimal path forward, even amidst challenges. It's about having the courage to make significant decisions while keeping our collective vision at the forefront of our minds, always considering what's best for the entire team. By steadfastly adhering to our strategy, we inch closer to our objectives and fortify our unity as a team.

A strategy serves as a bridge, linking the team's day-to-day efforts with the organisation's overarching vision and objectives. Imagine an orchestra playing in perfect harmony, where each note contributes to a breathtaking symphony. A clear strategy ensures that everyone comprehends how their individual contributions add to the larger picture, infusing their daily tasks with greater significance and alignment toward a shared purpose. It's the secret ingredient that ensures all efforts propel in unison, driving the organisation toward its aspirations.

This critical strategy doesn't materialise out of thin air; it begins at the helm of your organisation. It falls upon the leaders to craft this overarching plan and ensure its dissemination across every corner of your organisation, evolving into tailored strategies for each department or team. Think of it as a waterfall that flows from the top of a mountain, nourishing everything in its path. Leaders are responsible for ensuring that this flow reaches every branch, leaf and root, ensuring each team member understands how their contributions align with the organisation's overarching objectives. This top-down approach ensures that the organisational strategy isn't just a document gathering dust in a drawer but a living, breathing guide informing every company decision and action.

ALIGNMENT IS KEY

Alignment is the bedrock of strategic leadership, pivotal in guiding teams towards exceptional performance. Yet, the real hurdle often emerges from the misconception that alignment naturally exists, especially among senior teams. Despite genuine efforts, essential communications and strategies can veer off course, not due to negligence but underlying misalignments. I have seen this issue arise for many reasons:

- Leaders set different priorities or departmental goals that don't contribute to the overall goals;
- Organisations have a weak vision;
- Teams have an excess of goals, or, worst of all;
- There is no strategy, just a list of tactics.

Consequently, teams become busy yet unproductive, frustrated as efforts scatter in multiple directions.

THE ROLE OF STRATEGIC LEADERS

At the helm of every successful team stands a strategic leader, guiding the ship through turbulent waters towards the shores of organisational success. These leaders are not merely captains but visionaries who inspire and empower their teams to navigate challenges and achieve shared goals. Clarity of direction enables teams to make better decisions and adapt more effectively to the ever-changing demands of the business landscape.

Every brilliant team is led by a strategic thinker who understands the path forward, guiding their people through ups and downs to achieve remarkable feats together. These leaders are more than just guides; they are individuals who envision the bigger picture, rallying their teams to tackle challenges and reach goals collectively.

True leadership goes beyond overseeing work; it involves creating a compelling vision that inspires everyone to wholeheartedly follow. The best leaders strive to improve the lives of all involved, not solely focus on profits. They paint a vivid picture of what the organisation stands for, create team charters and guide everyone towards its goals. Particularly in challenging times, a strong vision can uplift morale and instil hope within the team.

Making tough decisions is an integral part of leadership. It requires an understanding of priorities and the ability to choose the best course of action. Strategic leaders navigate this terrain with precision, carefully weighing options and selecting the optimal path forward to ensure the team and company's success. However, leadership devoid of transparency, a clear vision and a meaningful purpose can lead to negative outcomes.

Leaders must transition from prioritising individual victories to championing the collective success of the organisation, fostering a culture of collaboration over competition. While many leaders may cling to a competitive mindset shaped by past experiences, genuine progress occurs when they recognise the value of achieving success together, redefining teamwork to prioritise collaboration, shared goals and mutual support.

Deciding on the best course of action often involves tough choices, like determining what's most important and what can wait. Being able to make these decisions confidently is a sign of true leadership. Strategic leaders understand the terrain, carefully consider their options and choose the best path forward to help the team and company succeed. But without honesty, a clear vision and a meaningful purpose, leadership can turn negative.

Achieving alignment requires ongoing effort and precision as the business landscape continually evolves. Strategies must adapt and be fine-tuned to remain ahead in the game. Yet, the effort is worth it. When a team unites under a shared goal, magic happens. Collaboration flourishes, creativity soars and success becomes not just possible but inevitable. Although challenging, strategic alignment is the key to unleashing your team's potential and marching towards triumph as one.

CRAFTING AN EFFECTIVE STRATEGY

Creating an effective strategy doesn't have to be complicated. In fact, I encourage you to keep it as simple as possible. The important factor is finding a path everyone on your team can follow and get excited about. Here are six simple steps to make sure your strategy hits the mark:

Start with 'Why': Revisit why your organisation exists. This 'Why' is your North Star, guiding everything from big decisions to daily tasks. Make sure your strategy connects directly to this purpose. It's what makes the work meaningful and keeps everyone motivated.

Set Clear Goals: Break down your vision into clear, achievable goals. These signposts on your journey show you're headed in the right direction. Each goal should be a stepping stone that moves you closer to your bigger picture.

Make it Relatable: Your strategy should speak to everyone, not just those in the boardroom. Use simple language and real-world examples to explain how each team member's work contributes to the goals, making the strategy a part of everyone's story.

Involve Your Team: Strategy isn't just a top-down decision. Involve your team in the planning process. This brings diverse perspectives and ensures that everyone feels ownership over the strategy. When people see their ideas reflected, they're more committed to making them happen.

Keep it Flexible: The business world changes fast. Your strategy should be adaptable, allowing room to pivot when necessary. Regular check-ins with your team can help you stay responsive and align your strategy with the reality on the ground.

Bring Your Strategy to Life: Remember, your strategy should be a living document, not something that gathers dust on a shelf. Make it a central part of your team meetings and daily conversations.

Regularly referencing and discussing your strategy ensures it stays relevant and at the top of everyone's mind. This approach keeps the strategy alive within the team, guiding decisions and actions. It becomes more than just a plan; it's the heartbeat of your team's journey towards success.

HOST A STRATEGY WORKSHOP

Hosting a team strategy workshop is a great way to bring fresh energy and focus to your team. While the concept may already be familiar, its potential impact is often underestimated. Hosting a workshop pulls the team out of the daily routine, creating a space dedicated to weaving the fabric of your long-term goals and strategies.

When facilitated well, one of the key strengths of a strategy workshop is its inclusive approach. The facilitator encourages everyone to participate, breaking down traditional hierarchies and giving a voice to those who might not usually speak up in a formal setting.

Great facilitators lead the sessions with great skill. These 'softer skills' – communication, collaboration, motivation – are becoming increasingly vital in the strategic planning process. Workshops allow team members to step into roles that contribute more dynamically to the strategy, acting as the driving force behind the organisation's objectives and ensuring alignment across the team.

Inviting experienced strategic consultants or facilitators to run the session can add invaluable perspectives. These external voices can challenge the usual ways of thinking and keep the strategy grounded and realistic. They can also critically assess your plans' assumptions and challenge industry norms that might need a fresh look. The nature of strategic planning is evolving, moving towards a more integrated approach that blends structured plans with the ability to adapt to unforeseen challenges and opportunities.

Workshops are perfect for developing these plans. They gather all the team's insights and offer a platform to bridge formal strategy with the agility to respond to spontaneous events. By involving the entire team in these sessions, the strategy becomes a shared vision everyone is committed to implementing. Adopting this less formal, more inclusive approach to strategic planning can significantly boost your organisation's ability to navigate the complexities of the modern world, making strategy workshops an invaluable tool in any leader's arsenal.

WHAT TO INCLUDE IN YOUR STRATEGY

Putting your strategy into action is about making it as clear and practical as possible.

- **Set Objectives**: Start with SMART goals that match your strategy – Specific, Measurable, Achievable, Relevant and Time-Bound goals.
- **Set Your Vision**: Next, craft a vision statement that pulls everyone in, giving your team something powerful to aim for.
- **Build Your Strategy** around three to five key areas or pillars and decide on the tactics to achieve them. Make sure everything you plan to do will help you reach your vision. The strategy house framework is a fantastic tool here; it helps you organise your strategy visually, making it easier to understand and follow.
- **Set Metrics**: Finally, set up Key Performance Indicators (KPIs) to monitor your progress and identify areas for improvement. This step-by-step approach ensures that your strategy isn't just a document – it's a living, breathing part of your team's daily life, guiding you all towards success.

CREATE A COMPELLING VISION

A compelling vision, paired with core values, is the anchor for effective leadership and strategy, offering organisational stability. The leader's foremost responsibility is articulating a vision that inspires and energises employees. This vision should align with the company's values to resonate with employees and garner their support.

The impact of vision and values statements cannot be overstated. Howard Schultz illustrated this principle with Starbucks, transforming it into a global brand by prioritising the creation of an integrity-based company and delivering exceptional coffee experiences to customers. Similarly, Google's vision statement, 'to provide access to the world's information in one click,' emphasises its commitment to clients and delineates its overarching global objective.

A desire for profit did not drive Google's inception, but dissatisfaction with existing search technology. Committed to crafting something superior, the company embarked on a mission to develop a new search engine. Today, Google commands an astounding 83.49% market share and facilitates over 8.5 billion daily searches, totalling a staggering 2 trillion searches per year worldwide. With an annual revenue surpassing $278 billion, Google's success is nothing short of extraordinary. Its mission statement – 'to organise and make knowledge universally obtainable and useful' – guides its strategies and endeavours to achieve its vision.

It is worth noting that there is a difference between mission and vision. While the vision statement outlines the company's direction, the mission statement clarifies its purpose. A thoughtfully crafted mission statement encapsulates the company's purpose and unique value proposition. Disney, for instance, is all about bringing joy and happiness to people.

Exceptional leaders recognise the importance of aligning the company's vision and mission, understanding that creating a compelling vision requires deliberate effort rather than leaving it to chance.

Strategy is indispensable in achieving team success, as exemplified by these mission and vision statements. Leaders establish strategic goals and objectives that delineate the company's trajectory, requiring deliberate and focused decision-making. With a clear vision, values and mission statements, teams have a guiding framework that informs their decision-making process.

When the team isn't united under a common purpose, dedication to shared objectives, efforts scatter and forward momentum grinds to a halt. A lack of team commitment deepens organisational challenges, leaving team members unsure and unaligned with mutual goals and priorities. Leaders stand at the forefront of turning this around by painting a clear and motivating vision, laying out explicit expectations and inspiring everyone to pull together towards a singular aim. This mission, vision and strategy become the beacon for teams to navigate these challenges, ensuring that every member is committed and passionately driven towards collective success.

SHORT- AND LONG-TERM GOALS

Goals are the milestones on your journey to success, shaping your daily challenges and victories. There are different types of goals to consider:

Short-term vs. Long-term Goals: Short-term goals are your immediate targets, which you plan to hit in the coming weeks or months. They're the steps you take today or this month. Long-term goals, however, are your vision for the future, taking a year or more to achieve. They're the strategic framework that guides the direction of your organisation over time.

Why Long-term Goals Matter: Long-term goals are essential because they outline your organisation's future direction. They involve detailed planning, setting milestones to celebrate progress, ensuring everyone knows their responsibilities, and consistent efforts year after year.

The Importance of Short-term Goals: Short-term goals have a dual role. Firstly, they address the immediate tasks or projects that need your attention now. Secondly, they act as checkpoints on the way to your bigger objectives. To reach a major milestone, you often need to break it down into smaller, more manageable parts.

SMART GOALS

Balancing short-term and long-term objectives with a collaborative planning approach is pivotal in steering your teams towards success amidst constant change. Whether you're a leader guiding a team or an individual striving for personal growth, setting clear and attainable goals is paramount. Whether short-term or long-term, make sure your goals are SMART.

To inspire and rally your team, it's crucial to strike the right balance between challenging and realistic goals. Setting unattainable objectives or ones that don't match your team's capabilities and resources serves no one. This is where the SMART goal framework proves invaluable. SMART, which stands for Specific, Measurable, Achievable, Relevant and Time-Bound, provides a structured approach to goal setting, breaking them down into actionable steps with defined timelines. Studies from McKinsey indicate that leveraging SMART goals can enhance productivity by up to 30%.[1]

By adhering to SMART principles, your goals remain clear, attainable and perfectly aligned with your overarching mission

---

1. McKinsey Report. Capturing the true value of industry four-point zero.

and values, ensuring that every effort contributes to your organisation's overarching success.

- **Specific**: Your goals should be clear, so your team knows exactly what to do.
- **Measurable**: Have ways to track your progress, whether through numbers or qualitative measures, so you can see how far you've come.
- **Achievable**: Aim for challenging but within-reach goals. Setting unrealistic targets can lead to frustration and disappointment.
- **Relevant**: Ensure your goals align with your organisation's objectives. This keeps everyone focused on the same mission.
- **Time-Bound**: Give yourself a deadline to create a sense of urgency and keep yourself accountable.

Think about your own goals for a moment. Are they SMART? Can you see a clear path from where you are now to where you want to be? Breaking your vision down into SMART goals can turn your aspirations into reality, step by achievable step.

SWOT AND STRATEGIC PILLARS

Incorporating a SWOT analysis into your strategic planning process is essential for identifying your organisation's strengths, weaknesses, opportunities and threats. This analysis is the foundation for developing strategic pillars that capitalise on strengths and opportunities while mitigating weaknesses and threats.

A strategic pillar is a cornerstone of your strategy, like a sturdy column supporting a structure. These pillars represent fundamental focus areas that drive achieving your long-term vision and goals. By aligning efforts and resources around these pillars, you can ensure that every action contributes to overall success.

Strategic pillars provide clarity and direction, organising initiatives and resources around key priorities. They guide decision-making processes and serve as a framework for measuring progress and outcomes. By defining clear strategic pillars informed by a SWOT analysis, you can effectively navigate challenges (the right ones, not every one!), leverage opportunities and stay aligned with their overarching strategic objectives.

Start by asking yourself: What critical success factors will get us to our vision? These might include innovation, customer satisfaction, operational efficiency or employee engagement. Effective strategies typically concentrate on no more than five pillars at a time, ensuring team focus remains sharp and workloads remain manageable. Attempting to juggle too many pillars can scatter team efforts and blur priorities, impeding cohesive progress.

Once you've pinpointed your strategic pillars, the next step is translating them into tactics. Tactics are the concrete steps you'll take to implement each strategic pillar. While a strategy establishes the course, tactics focus on execution. For each pillar, consider three to five actionable steps to bring the strategic pillar to fruition. For example, if one of your pillars is customer satisfaction, tactics might include:

- Implementing a new feedback system.
- Training your customer service team.
- Introducing a loyalty program.

Many teams rely solely on tactics, overlooking the importance of a strategic framework. This oversight often contributes to teams feeling overwhelmed and burnt out. Strategy provides clarity by indicating which tactics are essential to prioritise and which ones to discard. Just because a competitor implements a tactic doesn't necessarily mean it's the right approach for your organisation.

Remember, tactics should also be clear and measurable. They serve as the actionable steps that propel you towards your strategic objectives. You craft a visionary yet practical roadmap by delineating between the broader strokes of strategy and the detailed actions of tactics. This approach clarifies the path forward for your team and ensures that every endeavour contributes to achieving overarching goals. Access the strategic planning template I use at https://linktr.ee/bebrilliantconsultancy

SETTING CLEAR KPIS

Activities without measurable metrics lack effectiveness. Key Performance Indicators (KPIs) play a pivotal role for leaders and teams in comprehensively assessing performance. Brilliant teams recognise the importance of establishing measurable objectives to steer the organisation towards achievement. Clear KPIs are indispensable, providing a roadmap for performance and guiding teams towards their objectives with quantifiable benchmarks. They offer a holistic view of the company's performance by aligning business goals with tangible data within defined timeframes, facilitating informed decision-making, adjustments and performance enhancements along the way.

KPIs are tailored to each team's unique goals and requirements, varying from financial metrics to employee performance and operational indicators like customer acquisition or sales conversions. They provide real-time insights necessary for enhancing performance and achieving sustainable success. When establishing KPIs, leaders should focus on essential metrics that reflect team success, avoiding the pitfall of too many KPIs – it's about recognising the interconnectedness of different factors and identifying those critical for success. I always advocate for KPIs to be easily tracked in a single scorecard accessible to the team and visited in every meeting.

PLANNING CYCLE

Strategies require ongoing planning and monitoring for relevance and effectiveness. It's advisable to establish your strategy over a three-year horizon but to embrace flexibility by conducting annual reviews. Over one to two days each year, as a team, take the time to assess changes in the market and customer behaviour, ensuring your strategy remains aligned with these evolving dynamics.

To keep your annual strategy on track, commit to quarterly reviews. These sessions are crucial for making necessary adjustments, evaluating the progress of your goals and KPIs, and ensuring you're still heading in the right direction. You only need to spend a day at most to complete this.

Monthly meetings should examine the progress of your strategic pillars and priorities. Are they still relevant? Has anything changed? These regular check-ins help you stay focused on what remains important and ensure that every team member stays aligned with the overarching goals.

Dive into your tactics weekly. This is your opportunity to review the specific actions and initiatives driving your strategy forward. In these detailed discussions, you can see the pace of your progress and make swift adjustments as needed. Get your KPI scorecard out to check progress.

I've observed that employing this structured strategic planning and monitoring approach has led brilliant teams to make significant strides forward. By remaining vigilant and responsive to both internal and external changes, teams can sustain momentum and progress swiftly towards their objectives with precision and agility.

It's important to recognise that planning isn't a one-and-done task; it's an ongoing process of adaptation and refinement. It involves more than just setting goals; it's about operationalising your organisation's vision, purpose and values. This collaborative process integrates various perspectives and ideas, empowering teams to navigate the challenges of achieving their objectives in a dynamic and ever-evolving environment. Consider it a continuous journey rather than a one-time task.

YOUR BRILLIANT TEAM STRATEGY

When it comes to strategic leadership, your brilliant team will:

- Have clearly defined strategies.
- Have a robust planning cycle in place, with quarterly reviews
- Effectively plan short-term (one year).
- Effectively plan longer term (three to five years).
- Use a broad range of performance indicators (financial and non-financial) to set goals and review performance.

KEY TAKEAWAYS

- **Strategy is more than planning**; it involves navigating market changes, customer needs and competition to find opportunities and mitigate risk. Strategy provides direction and motivation and aligns actions with broader organisational goals.
- **A strong strategy ensures effective decision-making**, team alignment and a united path forward. Without a clear strategy, teams risk disorientation, inefficiency and disengagement.
- **Strategy begins at the top**, requiring leaders to develop and cascade it throughout the organisation to ensure

comprehensive alignment. Strategic leaders guide teams through challenges with a shared vision, fostering long-term value and a common purpose.

- **Alignment is crucial for strategic success.** It harmonises goals, actions and priorities with the organisational vision. It enables the organisation to accelerate its ambitions quicker than its competition.
- **Strategy workshops and planning cycles** are vital for adapting to the evolving strategic planning landscape. A proactive, inclusive approach to strategic planning, monitoring and adaptation ensures team alignment with the organisational vision and responsiveness to business dynamics.

2

ENCOURAGING NEW IDEAS

'I have not failed. I've just found ten thousand ways that won't work.'

— THOMAS EDISON

Businesses face ever-changing customer, supplier and workforce demands. What was relevant last year may no longer suffice as new technologies emerge and expectations evolve. Customers now seek quicker and easier solutions than ever before, placing a premium on teams' ability to continuously innovate and adapt.

Fostering a culture of innovation is paramount to thriving in this dynamic environment. It begins with leaders encouraging experimentation, risk-taking and open dialogue. When teams feel empowered to explore new ideas and approaches, they're more likely to uncover breakthrough innovations.

It's essential to remember that innovation takes various forms and each team member brings unique strengths to the table. Some excel at generating new ideas, while others specialise in refining and implementing them. Just like in sports, every team member plays a crucial role in driving collective success, emphasising collaboration and shared achievements over individual accomplishments.

WHAT IS TEAM INNOVATION?

Innovation means introducing new ideas, ways of doing things or solutions that really help people, teams or even bigger groups. It involves thinking outside the box and discovering improved methods to address challenges. For teams, fostering innovation means generating ideas that benefit the team, enhance the organisation as a whole and extend beyond its boundaries. Whether developing a new product, streamlining processes, or devising innovative solutions to existing problems, the goal is to deliver tangible value.

The essence of innovation lies in offering something genuinely fresh and valuable that hasn't been attempted before. It goes beyond mere novelty; it's about making a meaningful impact by addressing challenges innovatively. Innovation is about effectively implementing new ideas, continuously refining them and leveraging existing knowledge in novel ways.

THE SIGNIFICANCE OF INNOVATION WITHIN A TEAM

Do you ever feel like 'innovation' is just another corporate buzzword lacking significance in your daily routines? Well, it's time to debunk that myth. Innovation isn't just about boosting profits; it also fosters a sense of purpose among employees. When a company champions innovative thinking, risk-taking and experimentation, it injects new energy into the team. Employees become eager to contribute because they feel their ideas are valued and have room to experiment and innovate.

A workplace that embraces innovation becomes a magnet for creative minds seeking an environment that celebrates fresh ideas. Engaging in innovative projects can enhance job satisfaction and instil a sense of pride in team members' work, ultimately elevating morale and boosting overall engagement.

Innovation is essential for any organisation's survival in today's constantly evolving landscape. With technology advancing rapidly, research progressing swiftly and AI revolutionising traditional methods, innovation within teams becomes paramount for driving progress, maintaining competitiveness and fostering adaptability. By staying abreast of new trends and technologies, innovation ensures that teams remain ahead of the curve, avoiding the pitfalls of obsolescence. Moreover, it ignites creative approaches to problem-solving, yielding solutions that surpass the limitations of conventional methods.

Creating a culture of innovation goes beyond brainstorming sessions or inspirational posters; it requires fostering an environment where individuals feel empowered to take risks, viewing failure as an opportunity for growth rather than a setback. Additionally, innovation has the potential to unite team members by blending diverse skills and ideas, ultimately leading to superior outcomes. It enables teams to develop new products, enhance processes, and deliver value to both the company and its customers. Teams proficient in innovation exhibit agility in adapting to market shifts, technological advancements and evolving customer preferences, a vital attribute for sustaining long-term success.

THE GROWING INNOVATION GAP

Do people in your team feel free to dream, improve, innovate and be creative at work? According to Gallup research, only 29% of workers strongly agree that they are expected to be creative or think of new ways to do things at work[1]. When Gallup asked

---

1. Gallup. December 2018. Fostering Creativity at Work: Do Your Managers Push or Crush Innovation?

employees, 'What would you change about your workplace to make it better?', 41% said words in keeping with 'They should grant more autonomy in the work to stimulate everyone's creativity.'

An Adobe study on the case for creativity in the workplace revealed that 32% of employees don't feel comfortable thinking creatively in their current jobs[2].

WorkHuman reported in its 2019 International Employee Survey that companies have greater opportunities to 'leverage the previously untapped creativity and innovation of people – to prioritise humanity and emotional intelligence at work.'[3]

There is a growing gap between the demand for human creativity at work and the supply currently on offer. The World Economic Forum recently highlighted that creativity is one of the three most critical skills required to thrive in the twenty-first century and beyond[4]. Amazing advancements in technologies such as artificial intelligence, blockchain, virtual reality, nanotechnology, robotics and 3D/4D printing are poised to challenge individuals to engage in creative problem-solving and seize opportunities like never before.

Yet, Bloomberg research reported that creative problem-solving, communication, strategic thinking and leadership are the most desired but hardest-to-find skillsets[5].

With our newfound ability to digitally shape-shift time, space and matter (with tech like VR, augmented virtuality and the like), the age of limitless creative innovation is already upon us. Workers may already be aware of creative solutions to problems, but they

---

2. Adobe. How a Global Pandemic and Cultural Movements are Impacting the Industry.
3. WorkHuman Report. 2019. International Employee Survey.
4. World Economic Forum. May 2023. Future of Jobs Report.
5. Bloomberg Job Skills Report. 2015.

haven't been asked for their opinions or given the time to explore and experiment.

Businesses that don't prioritise innovation are at risk of lagging in productivity, customer satisfaction and market share. Without innovative ideas and novel approaches, companies become stagnant, causing their brands to lose relevance and making it difficult to attract new customers. If a team lacks innovation, creativity or new ideas, and there's no room for thinking and improving, several negative outcomes can occur:

Stagnation: The team's work and projects become stagnant, lacking freshness and excitement. This can lead to a drop in the quality of the team's output, as the same ideas and processes are recycled without improvement.

Loss of Competitive Edge: Without innovation, the team and, by extension, the organisation fall behind more dynamic and forward-thinking competitors. This results in losing market share, customers or opportunities to more innovative rivals.

Decreased Morale and Motivation: A stifling environment decreases morale among team members. When creativity is not encouraged or valued, team members feel their contributions are not appreciated, which decreases motivation and job satisfaction.

Talent Drain: Creative and innovative individuals are often driven by the opportunity to explore new ideas and approaches. If they feel their creativity is stifled, they seek opportunities elsewhere, resulting in the loss of talented staff.

Inflexibility: A lack of innovation creates a rigid and resistant team, which is detrimental in a rapidly evolving business environment. This inflexibility makes it difficult for the team to adapt to new challenges or changes in the market.

Missed Opportunities: Innovation often leads to discovering new opportunities, whether entering new markets, developing new products, or finding more efficient processes. Without creativity and innovation, these opportunities become overlooked.

Customer Dissatisfaction: In many industries, customers expect continuous improvement and innovation in products and services. A lack of innovation leads to customer dissatisfaction and erodes loyalty as customers turn to other providers who can meet their evolving needs.

To prevent these negative outcomes, you must foster an environment that encourages innovation and creativity, where team members feel safe sharing new ideas and where there is a continuous push for improvement and excellence.

ESTABLISHING AN INNOVATION CULTURE

Teams that innovate possess several key characteristics: They support new ideas, are dedicated to common goals, prioritise excellence and, importantly, foster an environment where everyone feels comfortable sharing and contributing.

A culture of innovation begins with effective leadership. Leaders should cultivate an environment that promotes experimentation, welcomes risks and failures and allows for open communication. Significant breakthroughs occur when teams are empowered to take risks and think creatively.

It's important to remember that individuals may have different approaches to the creative process. Some are skilled at generating ideas, while others are exceptional at refining or putting them into action. And that is okay – indeed, it is crucial for constructing a brilliant team. As in sports, each team member plays a crucial part in attaining success. The focus is on collective achievement rather than personal recognition, and the team strives to exceed limitations.

Creativity thrives in an atmosphere encouraging open-mindedness and positivity, where peers are supportive and collaborative rather than critical and confrontational. Teams that lack cohesion or prefer to work independently may also miss out on the opportunity to share fresh ideas and ignite creative inspiration. This is especially important when individuals are frequently required to perform under high pressure. To foster innovation, teams must devote ample time to exploring various ideas and perspectives without getting caught up in unnecessary disagreements. Finding more effective ways to express emotions while still standing ground when disagreements arise would be helpful.

STRATEGIES TO CULTIVATE AND ELEVATE INNOVATION

Have you ever had an epic idea? If so, think about where you were. Many people find inspiration while walking their dog, showering or driving. Our best ideas come when we can craft a space that ignites creativity. This could mean having a special spot just for brainstorming or letting your team have downtime for chit-chat. Letting your mind drift can spark those 'aha' moments. Sometimes, the best ideas come when we least expect them, so don't be afraid to let your team step back and let their thoughts roam free.

Gallup research reveals that fostering a work culture that encourages creativity while providing sufficient time and freedom to take risks significantly increases the percentage of workers who feel empowered to innovate, from 20% to 70%.[6]

And the freedom to explore is invaluable. Experiments, even those that fail, are essential to success, as failures invariably lead to new

---

6. Gallup. Dec 2018. Fostering creativity at work.

insights and learning opportunities. Here are a few ideas to get your team's innovative juices flowing:

Encourage open and judgment-free brainstorming sessions. These sessions can generate new ideas and solutions in person or virtually. Often, the best ideas are a blend of different thoughts or a simple concept with a twist.

Cross-departmental collaboration can also fuel creativity by bringing together diverse perspectives and insights. Don't hesitate to seek input from colleagues in different areas of expertise or use creative problem-solving techniques.

Taking calculated risks and embracing unconventional thinking can lead to exciting outcomes.

Investing in ongoing education and training opportunities can help team members expand their skills and perspectives. And don't forget to reward and celebrate creativity – it's a powerful motivator for seeking new solutions and achieving goals.

Finally, **embracing diversity** in your team can bring fresh viewpoints and ideas to the table. Fostering an inclusive environment and exploring ideas from various sectors can fuel innovation and help your team stay ahead of the curve.

LEADERSHIP ACTIVITIES THAT FOSTER TEAM INNOVATIVENESS

Leaders must lead by example to inspire innovation within their teams. Demonstrating a readiness to explore new possibilities, develop ideas and embrace experimentation can inspire employees to think creatively and push beyond their comfort zones. In today's competitive business landscape, nurturing a culture where innovation is prized is essential for maintaining a competitive edge.

Moreover, leaders should foster openness and inclusivity by involving their teams in decision-making processes. Sharing information and soliciting input demonstrates to employees that their perspectives are valued, encouraging them to engage more actively. By stimulating creativity through challenges and encouraging teams to devise new solutions, leaders can unlock the full potential of their teams.

It's equally important to grant teams the autonomy to manage their projects and learn from mistakes while providing support and guidance along the way. This approach empowers teams to turn innovative ideas into tangible outcomes, thereby adding value to the organisation.

CONTINUOUS IMPROVEMENT

Leaders should cultivate an environment where new ideas are embraced and failure is regarded as a stepping stone toward continuous improvement. Innovation extends beyond groundbreaking concepts to encompass ongoing efforts to better engage customers, enhance product quality and streamline processes.

Recognising both successes and areas for improvement is crucial, as is learning from each experience. Encouraging teams to explore why certain ideas didn't yield the expected results allows for refinement and growth rather than premature dismissal. By dedicating time to assess and enhance, leaders can instil a culture where continuous improvement propels the team forward, aligns departments, fosters collaboration and ensures responsiveness to evolving market and customer needs.

It's important to understand that deriving value from every endeavour, regardless of its outcome, is not wasteful but foundational to fostering sustained innovation and growth.

KEY METRICS FOR INNOVATION

So, what exactly should you be measuring? Here are some key metrics to consider:

- **Number of New Ideas Generated:** The quantity of ideas produced. It's a starting point for measuring innovation, but quantity must be balanced with quality.
- **Percentage of Time Spent on Innovation Activities:** This measures commitment. How much of our time is dedicated to thinking outside the box? Are we carving out enough space for creativity?
- **Rate of Idea Implementation:** It's not just the ideas we generate; it's the ones we bring to life that count. This metric looks at how many ideas become reality.

These metrics serve as evaluation tools and sources of inspiration. They will inspire you to push boundaries and approach challenges with a fresh perspective. By tracking ideas, conducting audits and analysing metrics, you're laying the groundwork for a more innovative future.

BRILLIANT TEAMS AND INNOVATION

When it comes to innovation, your brilliant team will:

- Always be looking to add new value and deliver better results.
- Constantly improve key processes.
- Be creative and think outside the box.
- Regularly implement new ideas.
- Regularly talk about long-term, new opportunities.

KEY TAKEAWAYS

- **Innovation Beyond Novelty:** Innovation doesn't always mean inventing something entirely new. It can involve implementing novel ideas or approaches, even if they're not entirely original. This broader perspective allows businesses to improve processes, products and services, fostering continuous improvement and adaptation.
- **Long-Term Sustainability Through Innovation:** Innovation is not just desirable; it's essential for long-term sustainability. Businesses that fail to innovate risk becoming stagnant and outdated in a rapidly evolving market. By continuously innovating, businesses can stay ahead of the curve, anticipate market trends and meet evolving customer needs.
- **Risk of Falling Behind:** Failure to innovate can have serious consequences for businesses. In today's competitive landscape, staying stagnant is not an option. Businesses that fail to innovate risk falling behind their rivals, losing market share, and alienating clients and stakeholders. Innovation is crucial for maintaining relevance and competitiveness in a dynamic market environment.
- **Leadership in Creating an Innovative Climate:** Leaders play a pivotal role in fostering an innovation environment within their organisations. They must create a culture that encourages creativity, experimentation and risk-taking. By providing support, resources and encouragement for innovation initiatives, leaders set the tone for the entire organisation and inspire their teams to think innovatively.
- **Employee Satisfaction and Motivation:** Employee satisfaction and motivation are essential to innovation. When employees feel valued, empowered and engaged,

they are more likely to contribute their ideas and take initiative in driving innovation. Leaders must create a work environment that fosters collaboration, encourages diverse perspectives and rewards innovation.

3

STAYING ACCOUNTABLE

'Great things in business are never done by one person; they're done by a team of people.'

— STEVE JOBS

Accountability is the glue that ties commitment to performance – taking responsibility for your actions, your impact on the team and your goals. When everyone in a team knows what they're responsible for and commits to it, magic happens. Projects move smoothly, deadlines are met and the atmosphere buzzes with progress energy. But accountability isn't just about ticking boxes on a task list; it's about owning the journey towards a shared vision. It means saying, 'I've got this,' and meaning it, ensuring that your puzzle piece fits perfectly into the bigger picture.

WHAT IS ACCOUNTABILITY?

Accountability is at the core of our team dynamics. It embodies respect for our commitments, our colleagues and the collective vision we're pursuing. Accountability is more than just task completion; it's about taking pride in our work and recognising our role in the team's triumphs. When we embrace accountability, we're not just fulfilling obligations but contributing to something greater than ourselves, something truly remarkable.

Accountability means doing what you should do and being responsible for the outcomes. It means everyone understands and takes responsibility for their actions, decisions and work outcomes. Team members are reliable and follow through on commitments. Roles are clearly defined; expectations are explicit and individuals feel empowered to deliver results. Trust permeates the culture, fostering a sense of support and acknowledging that every contribution matters. Alignment towards common goals is natural and challenges are met openly and constructively, focusing on growth and progress.

Teams that commit to decisions and standards of performance do not hesitate to hold one another accountable for adhering to those decisions and standards. What is more, they don't rely on the team leader as the primary source of accountability; instead, they go directly to their peers. They hold each other to the decisions and standards they've collectively agreed upon. This team accountability is the glue that binds the team together and propels them towards shared objectives. It's about fostering trust and camaraderie, both through spoken rules and unspoken collaboration, creating an environment where success is shared, and challenges are faced together.

While this approach may not solve every problem, it unites and keeps focus on the mission. The team is driven by personal success and a collective desire to excel. Trust and a sense of belonging are foundational, laying the groundwork to tackle even greater challenges as a cohesive unit.

WHEN ACCOUNTABILITY IS MISSING

Imagine a boat where everyone's supposed to be rowing, but some aren't pulling their weight. The result? The boat spins in circles, progress stagnates and frustration mounts. Lack of accountability breeds missed opportunities, duplicated efforts and failure to achieve collective goals. When accountability wanes, deadlines slip, blame-shifting abounds and excuses become the norm. We've all encountered individuals who seem perpetually overwhelmed, avoiding responsibility at every turn, right?

This cycle often leads to learned helplessness – a belief that one can't alter their circumstances due to past failures or seemingly insurmountable challenges. It's like hitting a wall repeatedly, only to conclude that progress is impossible. Such feelings of stagnation can breed a sense of resignation, hindering efforts to effect change or seek improvement. The absence of feedback or constant rejection can exacerbate this sensation, creating a self-perpetuating cycle of frustration and inertia.

Working in an environment devoid of trust and accountability is like being part of a team without rules. In the absence of regulations, chaos reigns.

DEVELOPING A CULTURE OF ACCOUNTABILITY

So, how do we build a culture of accountability? It starts with clear expectations from you, the leader. Make sure everyone knows what they need to do and when.

- Keep the lines of communication open with regular updates and check-ins.
- Create a supportive space where your team can take risks and learn from mistakes without fear of blame.
- Role model what accountability looks like.
- Celebrate your team's wins.

- Tackle challenges in a way that's open and positive.
- Encourage your team to challenge the lack of accountability.

Remember, challenging accountability isn't about finding fault – it's about supporting each other, learning together and moving forward as a united team. Teamwork, accountability and collaboration are the heart of achieving success.

Set The Example: Leaders should show responsibility in their actions, decisions and communication. This involves acknowledging and taking responsibility for errors, openly discussing difficulties and fulfilling promises. Leaders play a crucial role in setting the tone for the entire team by demonstrating accountability.

Setting Clear Expectations: Establishing clear expectations is fundamental to fostering team accountability. For leaders, this entails transparently communicating goals, success criteria and desired behaviours. Despite these efforts, ambiguity surrounding roles and tasks can still arise, resulting in conflicts and incomplete work. Leaders may assume that employees inherently understand their roles and expect them to uphold high standards and actively contribute ideas. However, lacking clear guidance, employees may find it challenging to meet these expectations.

Concerns about appearing overly demanding might lead leaders to refrain from setting explicit expectations, leaving employees uncertain about the standards of excellence. Effective communication is paramount in this regard, necessitating leaders to be direct and consistent in articulating expectations. This might mean repeating messages to ensure they're understood and embraced. Clarity boosts individual accountability, making employees more receptive to feedback and reducing resistance to performance evaluations based on unclear standards.

Encouraging Ownership: Encouraging ownership among employees can lead to better job outcomes. Employees who believe they can handle their work well are more likely to take on challenges and find effective solutions. This sense of self-belief boosts individual performance and makes the whole team more effective. Teams confident in their abilities are open to trying new things, which can lead to happier customers and more dedicated employees.

Instead of closely controlling every task, leaders should empower their team members. This is especially important for newer employees who show they can take ownership. To build a workplace where everyone feels empowered, leaders should focus on:

- Sharing responsibility and letting others make decisions.
- Including team members in making important choices.
- Trusting team members to do their jobs well.
- Making work feel meaningful and important to everyone.

BELBIN'S TEAM ROLES

Defining team roles and responsibilities often brings the best results, especially in diverse teams. Team roles outline how people act, contribute and interact within a group, shaping the team's overall performance. Dr. Meredith Belbin's team roles theory identifies nine roles that individuals can assume within a team, each contributing to the team's success in unique ways. These roles contribute to fostering a balanced team and enhancing accountability, as each member's responsibilities are clear and aligned with their strengths. Here's a brief overview of how these roles contribute to accountability:

Shaper (SH): This person energises the team to overcome obstacles, focusing on goals and pushing the team forward. Their drive ensures the team remains motivated and on track, contributing to a culture of accountability for achieving team objectives.

Implementer (IMP): Turns ideas into actionable tasks with a practical, organised approach, ensuring that plans are executed efficiently. Their focus on implementation keeps the team grounded and accountable to timelines and standards.

Completer-Finisher (CF): This role pays attention to detail and ensures nothing is overlooked, helping the team meet its commitments with high-quality outputs. It is crucial to hold the team accountable to quality standards and deadlines.

Coordinator (CO): Acts as a chairperson, guiding the team's decision-making process and ensuring effective communication. By clarifying goals and roles, the Coordinator fosters accountability by aligning team efforts with the project's objectives.

Team Worker (TW): This person supports team members and fosters a positive team spirit. They help maintain a collaborative and accountable team environment and ensure that all members are engaged and contributing effectively.

Resource Investigator (RI): This person explores external opportunities and brings fresh ideas to the team. Their role in networking and gathering resources keeps the team innovative and accountable for exploring all avenues for success.

Plant (PL) Provides creative and innovative solutions to complex problems. Their creative thinking encourages the team to explore new approaches, holds the team accountable for innovation and does not settle for the status quo.

Monitor Evaluator (ME): Offers critical analysis and strategic insights, ensuring that the team's plans are feasible and goals are realistic. Their analytical approach fosters accountability by preventing oversight and ensuring decisions are well-grounded.

Specialist (SP): This person brings in-depth knowledge of a specific area to the team, ensuring that the team's actions are informed and credible. Their expertise holds the team accountable for maintaining high standards of professionalism and accuracy.

By understanding and leveraging these roles, teams can create a more accountable and effective working environment. Ideally, a balanced team has a mix of all nine roles, ensuring a range of skills and approaches. However, perfect balance is rare, so knowing which roles are underrepresented or missing and who might unexpectedly fill them is beneficial. As teams gain experience and self-awareness, their understanding of roles can evolve, improving communication and meeting team goals more effectively. Sharing responsibilities and understanding each other's roles can greatly enhance a team's efficiency and cohesion.

HOLDING EACH OTHER ACCOUNTABLE:

Accountability avoidance represents a stumbling block for teams, as members may shirk responsibility or fail to hold themselves and others to high-performance standards. By establishing clear roles, responsibilities and performance metrics, teams can create a culture of accountability where individuals take ownership of their actions and outcomes, driving continuous improvement and results. Embracing accountability in the workplace is essential for building trust, promoting collaboration and working together toward shared objectives.

Teams dedicated to making decisions and maintaining high-performance standards are not afraid to hold each other accountable for following through on those decisions and standards. In addition, they don't depend on the team leader for accountability; instead, they approach their peers directly. When accountability within a team is successfully implemented, it shows:

- Individuals are held accountable by team members for their behaviour and conduct.
- Individuals are held accountable by the team for outcomes.
- Peer feedback supports and challenges others.
- Team members provide productive feedback to each other.
- When the team underperforms, team members challenge each other to improve.

THE RACI MODEL

The RACI model is a tool I use frequently with clients. It's a simple framework that keeps teams accountable by clearly outlining who does what in a project. RACI stands for:

- **Responsible**: The person who does the work to complete the task.
- **Accountable**: The person ultimately answerable for the correct and thorough task completion.
- **Consulted**: People who provide input based on their expertise before the task is done and who may be impacted by the work.
- **Informed**: Those who are kept up-to-date on progress, often only after actions or decisions are made.

The RACI model offers a simple and efficient method for ensuring clarity and alignment within teams. It establishes clear roles and responsibilities, ensures that tasks are delegated to the appropriate individuals and facilitates transparency regarding who is ultimately accountable for the final outcome.

Implementing the RACI model helps streamline decision-making processes, mitigating the frustration associated with committee decisions and preventing micro-management. Moreover, it fosters a sense of ownership among team members by clearly defining their roles and empowering them to take ownership of their responsibilities.

By embracing accountability, facilitating clear communication and leveraging tools such as the RACI model, you enhance the effectiveness and cohesion of your teams, ultimately driving progress and success.

For more details on RACI and to download a RACI Matrix template, visit https://linktr.ee/bebrilliantconsultancy

CONSTRUCTIVE FEEDBACK

Feedback plays a crucial role in keeping teams on track and accountable. Constructive feedback serves as a guiding light, steering individuals in the right direction. Additionally, positive feedback can provide a motivational boost, encouraging continued progress. But not all feedback feels great. Sometimes, activities may not go to plan and feedback is needed to enable course corrections.

Navigating the realm of feedback requires finesse. It's not solely about what is communicated but also how and when it's delivered. The best kind of feedback helps you grow. It points out what you're good at and where you can improve. Clear goals and understanding expectations are pivotal in leveraging feedback, particularly when venturing into uncharted territory.

Additionally, the source of feedback matters, whether from a superior, colleague or self-assessment. Feedback should be supportive and constructive, fostering a culture of learning and development.

In a team built on a foundation of trust, feedback becomes a catalyst for improvement. It's viewed as a collaborative effort to advance collective goals rather than an indictment of individual performance. It's not seen as criticism but a method to help each other improve. This way, feedback becomes a tool for growth, not a source of fear or tension.

By championing accountability and providing a supportive environment for feedback exchange, leaders cultivate a culture conducive to high performance and success.

BRILLIANT TEAMS AND ACCOUNTABILITY

When it comes to accountability, your brilliant team will:

- Hold each other accountable for their behaviour and conduct.
- Hold each other accountable for outcomes.
- Use peer feedback to support and challenge each other.
- Provide effective feedback to each other.
- Challenge each other to improve when the team underperforms.

KEY TAKEAWAYS

- **Clear Expectations:** Setting clear and achievable expectations is the foundation of accountability. When team members understand what is expected of them, they are better equipped to align their efforts with organisational goals and take responsibility for their tasks.
- **Accountability Unites Effort and Commitment**: Embracing accountability means fully owning our roles and creating a vibrant, progress-driven environment where everyone is committed to the shared vision and their part in achieving it.
- **Respect and Pride in Work Fuel Accountability**: Owning our tasks isn't just about meeting expectations; it's about respecting our commitments, our team and the collective

goals we're aiming for. This pride in our contributions fosters a powerful sense of accountability.

- **Role Modelling Sets the Tone**: Leaders are critical in demonstrating accountability, setting a positive example through their actions and decisions and fostering an environment where mistakes are seen as growth opportunities.

- **Feedback is a Cornerstone of Improvement**: Constructive feedback, given from a place of trust and aimed at growth, helps teams adjust, improve and stay aligned with their objectives.

4

CHANGE LEADERSHIP

'It is not the strongest or the most intelligent of the species that survives, but the one most responsive to change.'

— CHARLES DARWIN

Change is the only constant in today's fast-paced business landscape. It isn't merely a challenge to overcome but drives evolution. According to a recent PwC Survey, leaders anticipate an average of six major organisational changes within the next three years[1]. 82% acknowledge that these changes demand complex thinking and innovative solutions for success. The workplace is undergoing a multitude of transformations, including the integration of AI, the convergence of five generations, digital advancements, sustainability initiatives, economic crises and much more.

Successful change leadership goes beyond keeping the ship afloat; it involves charting a course toward new horizons, motivating everyone on board and securing the company's future prosperity.

---

1. PwC. Thriving in an age of continuous reinvention.

NETFLIX: A SUCCESS STORY IN LEADING CHANGE

Netflix began as a humble mail-order DVD rental service that thrived in the early 2000s. However, the rise of digital streaming technology signalled a seismic shift on the horizon. Rather than clinging to their traditional business model, Netflix's executive leadership foresaw the impending change and chose to embrace it rather than close their eyes and cling to their existing business model.

The pivot to streaming was not just a shift in service delivery; it represented a complete transformation of their business model. Transitioning from mailing DVDs to streaming content online required technological innovation, a cultural shift within the company and a re-education of its customer base.

CEO Reed Hastings played a pivotal role in this transformation. He championed the streaming model and guided the company through its uncertainties. Clear communication, unwavering commitment to the new strategy and the willingness to invest resources in uncharted territory were key factors in Netflix's successful transition.

And Netflix didn't stop there. They revolutionised the industry once again by producing original content. Their groundbreaking series House of Cards marked the beginning of Netflix as a distributor and entertainment creator, competing directly with established networks and studios. Today, Netflix is a leading force in the entertainment industry, boasting millions of subscribers worldwide.

The success of Netflix's digital transformation is a powerful example of effective leadership in times of change. It demonstrates how foresight, courage and unwavering commitment can navigate change and leverage it as a catalyst for growth and innovation. As we explore further in this chapter, the principles applied by

Netflix's leaders can serve as inspiration for guiding your team through the winds of change.

UNDERSTANDING CHANGE

What is your first reaction when you hear the word 'change'? It's a word that often invokes a mix of emotions, from excitement to apprehension. Change within an organisation is as inevitable as the tide, with its peaceful waves and stormy surges. It can come from any direction and take many forms, challenging leaders to navigate through calm waters and turbulent seas alike. Great leaders don't just ride the waves of change; they anticipate and prepare accordingly, much like Netflix's leadership did. Understanding the nature and drivers of change is essential for effective leadership through tumultuous times.

Let's face it, change is everywhere! Whatever your reaction to change is, you can't escape it. All kinds of changes are afoot. If you are a leader, you're undoubtedly right in the midst of change as you read this book. Various transformations are underway, each demanding adept leadership for success. Some leaders are revitalising team engagement amid dwindling motivation, while others are orchestrating a return to the office environment and manoeuvring hybrid work arrangements. Additionally, leaders guide their teams through transitions prompted by shifting market and business landscapes. In this dynamic environment, effective leadership is essential across all change fronts.

In the workplace, change manifests in various ways, from major events like mergers and acquisitions to market trend shifts, new competitors' arrival or technological advancements driving digital transformations. Even the introduction of new team members or leadership changes can spark change. While change may provoke uncertainty, it's a natural part of progress and evolution. Change leadership goes beyond management; it guides teams and organisations through transitions and challenges, fostering adaptability and growth.

Picture the business world as a dynamic ecosystem where adaptation is essential for survival. Embracing change isn't just a choice; it's a necessity. By embracing change, we unlock opportunities for innovation, expansion and continuous learning, viewing it as a catalyst for progress rather than a hurdle to overcome.

Yes, change can be tough. It can mean stepping out of your comfort zone, facing uncertainty and sometimes, meeting resistance. But with the right approach – clear planning, open communication, and strong leadership – you can move through change smoothly, turning challenges into chances to shine.

When faced with new competitors, companies can reassess their strategies, innovate and emerge stronger than before. It's an opportunity to cultivate a team that is agile, open to learning and capable of adapting to new challenges. Effectively navigating change requires careful planning, clear communication and strong leadership to ensure a smooth transition.

Change opens doors to innovation, creativity and growth. It allows you to reassess your strategies, realign your goals and explore new avenues for development.

KOTTER'S CHANGE MODEL

John P. Kotter's work on change management is legendary. His eight-step model is still the go-to resource for change management. It has stood the test of time, providing a reliable framework for organisations navigating transitions.

Because of its proven success, I'll only briefly touch upon it here. Our discussion will focus on how leaders can effectively guide their teams through the process of change, drawing on the principles behind Kotter's model while emphasising the leadership and team behaviours that make the difference. Instead, we will delve into how to implement changes in both structure and processes, as well as in the team's culture, ensuring that every team member is engaged, empowered and aligned towards the collective goals. This approach contributes to the essential elements of leading a brilliant team, where change leadership is pivotal in driving success.

Here are the stages that Kotter recommended:

Establish Urgency: Kick off the process by highlighting the need for change. This creates a preliminary sense of importance that can help motivate your team to take action.

Create a Guided Coalition: Form a strong coalition of change leaders. This team should have the right mix of skills and influence to guide the change effort effectively.

Develop a Vision and Strategy: Craft a clear vision and strategy for the change. This will give everyone a sense of direction and outline how to achieve the goals.

Communicate the Change Vision: Communicate the vision clearly and often so that every team member understands and is aligned with the change.

Empower Broad-Based Action: Remove obstacles that could impede change and empower others to act on the vision by changing systems or structures that undermine the change vision.

Generate Short-Term Wins: Plan for and celebrate visible, significant successes early on. Short-term wins can build momentum and increase buy-in.

Consolidate Gains and Produce More Change: Use the credibility gained from early wins to tackle bigger and deeper changes, ensuring the change process builds on itself.

Anchor New Approaches in the Culture: Make sure the changes are seen as part of corporate success and embedded in the culture. This helps solidify the change and ensure it's part of the organisation long-term.

This framework can greatly assist leaders in steering their teams through the complex change landscape, ensuring a collaborative and effective approach to transformation.

THE ROLE OF LEADERS IN MANAGING CHANGE

While there is a proven process for leading change, what often remains unexplored is the nuanced task of guiding the team through the psychological and behavioural challenges that arise during change when emotions are high and fear is present. A leader's role extends beyond orchestrating the change process; it involves shepherding the team through the journey, ensuring their emotional and psychological well-being every step of the way. Effective leadership isn't about dragging or coercing the team through change; it's about fostering understanding, empathy and support to minimise casualties and maximise success.

Leading change is certainly more than just making decisions; you must illuminate the path forward, demonstrate empathy and unite everyone to navigate change collectively. Change is a big part of our work today. It can be tough, but it's also a chance for individual and collective growth. You have a big job in making change work, ensuring everyone knows where they're heading, why change is happening, and how each person contributes.

Honesty is key. You should be transparent about why change is needed and what's expected. Be honest. Share why change is necessary and what's expected. This builds trust, reduces conspiracy theories and resistance and fosters inclusivity. Encourage team members to share their thoughts and feelings to boost commitment. Help your team adapt by providing support, tools and encouragement to tackle new challenges. Take charge of change proactively, setting clear goals, involving your team and offering solid support. This way, you don't just get through change; you make the most of it, turning challenges into opportunities to shine.

DEALING WITH RESISTANCE TO CHANGE

Change is inevitable. Yet, despite its certainty, it can be challenging to embrace. As human beings, we have an innate dislike of change and often, our initial response is to resist or reject it. However, in the workplace, this resistance is not a viable solution. When confronted with significant organisational transformations, change fatigue can quickly take hold. This fatigue may manifest in various forms, from decreased engagement and persistent complaints to elevated levels of absenteeism and attrition. Change can elicit a myriad of emotions, ranging from excitement and anticipation to fear and uncertainty. This fear and uncertainty often give rise to resistance – a natural response to anything that disrupts the status quo.

Why do people resist change? Well, there are several common reasons, but the most prevalent is the fear of the unknown and the loss of control.

The 'unknown' is a powerful force that can immobilise many individuals. One of the greatest fears people face when confronted with change is how it will personally impact them. Questions such as 'Will I lose my job?' or 'What will my role look like after the change?' can evoke significant anxiety and resistance. Uncertainty about the future can amplify these concerns, leading to apprehension and opposition among those struggling to navigate the ambiguity.

Similarly, the feeling of not being in control often contributes to resistance. Change frequently entails relinquishing familiar routines and processes, which can be unsettling for individuals who value autonomy. Some may worry about their ability to adapt or feel marginalised by decisions made without their input. The loss of autonomy can breed resentment and resistance as individuals strive to regain control over their circumstances.

Gaining insight into employees' resistance to change is the initial step in effectively addressing and overcoming it. By empathising with your team's concerns and fears, you can begin to develop strategies to assist them in navigating the upcoming change more smoothly. Addressing your team's concerns requires active listening and communication. Start by openly discussing the reasons behind the change and its implications for everyone involved. Keeping everyone informed reduces the fear of uncertainty.

Engage your team by involving them in the change process. Encourage their input and feedback to foster a sense of ownership and commitment to the changes.

Provide support throughout the transition through training, mentorship or simply being available to answer questions. Utilise your organisation's communications team to ensure everyone stays connected and informed, boosting confidence and facilitating success.

BUILDING RESILIENCE AND ADAPTABILITY

Prepare your team for change and equip them with the resilience to overcome challenges. Later in the book, I have dedicated a full chapter on resilience, but in short, in times of change, you must support your teams in understanding that challenges are chances to grow, not reasons to give up.

To do this, you must encourage a growth mindset. This means celebrating effort, learning from mistakes and understanding that our abilities aren't fixed; we can always get better with practice and persistence. It's about saying, 'We might not be able to do this yet, but with time and effort, we will.'

Promote a culture of continuous learning within your team. Encourage curiosity, create an environment where questions are welcomed and foster a thirst for new knowledge. This cultivates adaptability and readiness to face any situation.

As a leader, champion resilience among your team members. Provide support, offer guidance and remind them of their strengths during setbacks. Demonstrating resilience in the face of adversity helps manage change effectively. It transforms your team into a dynamic group of learners, innovators and problem-solvers, poised for the future.

EVALUATING SUCCESS AND CONTINUOUS IMPROVEMENT

The journey doesn't end once change has been implemented. That's just the beginning of a new chapter – one where you evaluate success and continuously strive for improvement. So, how do you measure success in the wake of change, and how do you keep up the momentum?

Measuring success during and after implementation requires a multifaceted approach. I recommend looking at more than your bottom-line numbers or ticking boxes from a list of activities. Instead, try evaluating the impact of those changes on the organisation, its people and its overall performance.

One key aspect of measuring success is assessing how well the changes align with the organisation's goals and objectives. Ask yourself (and the team), 'Are we moving closer to achieving our vision?' 'Are we meeting the needs of our customers and stakeholders?' These will help guide the effectiveness of your implemented changes.

Setting milestones and tracking progress is akin to mapping out a journey – it illustrates how far you've come and keeps the team focused on the destination. Here are a few strategies to uplift and motivate your team while measuring progress:

Break It Down: Break down the change process into smaller, manageable pieces. These are your milestones – key points along the way that signify progress.

Make It Measurable: Decide how you'll know each milestone has been reached. Will it be completing a part of a project, hitting a specific target, or achieving a particular outcome? Being clear about this will make it easier to see progress.

Celebrate the Small Wins: Celebrate every milestone reached! These celebrations boost morale and show the team that their hard work makes a difference. It's not just about the big, end goal; it's about recognising the effort and achievements along the way.

Keep Everyone Informed: Regularly share updates on progress towards milestones. This keeps everyone in the loop, reinforces the sense of a shared mission and can inspire those involved to keep pushing forward.

Adjust as Needed: Sometimes, you'll need to adjust milestones based on what you're learning along the way. That's okay. It's part of staying flexible and responsive to the change process.

By setting milestones and measuring progress, you're not just navigating change but acknowledging every step of growth and improvement. This approach demonstrates that change is not just possible; it's happening, one win at a time. Celebrating these wins will reinforce your commitment to the journey and highlight the tangible benefits of your collective efforts.

Success isn't just about outcomes; it's about the whole journey. It's about how well you've engaged your team members, communicated with them and supported them through the changes. Are your team members satisfied and motivated? Are they embracing the changes and contributing positively to the organisation's goals? Their feedback and satisfaction are crucial indicators of success.

Remember, leading change in your team isn't just about them knowing it's happening; it's about getting them actively involved, encouraging them to look for ways to improve, keeping the energy up and striving for greatness together.

SUSTAINING CHANGE

Sustaining change is like maintaining a garden – it requires regular care, attention and adjustments to thrive over time. Here are a few ways that you can ensure that the changes you've worked so hard to implement take root and grow within your team's culture and operations:

- **Provide Ongoing Support:** Just as plants need water to grow, our teams need ongoing support to adapt to new ways of working. This might mean continuing training, providing resources or simply being there to answer questions and offer guidance.
- **Reinforce New Behaviours:** Acknowledge and celebrate when team members demonstrate the desired behaviours. This positive reinforcement makes it clear that these new ways of working are valued and appreciated, encouraging others to follow suit.
- **Be Open to Feedback:** Change isn't always smooth, and feedback is like the soil feedback that nourishes growth. Encourage your team to share their thoughts on what's working and what isn't. This open dialogue can uncover valuable insights for fine-tuning the change process.
- **Adjust Based on Feedback:** Just as a gardener adjusts their approach based on the weather and the needs of their

plants, be prepared to make adjustments based on the feedback you receive. This shows your team that you're committed to making the change work for everyone and that you are listening!

- **Embed Change into the Culture:** Make change a part of your team's story. Share success stories, incorporate the new ways into your team rituals and routines, and ensure new team members are introduced to these practices from the start. Over time, the change will become a natural part of your team's operations.

By providing ongoing support, reinforcing new behaviours, listening to and acting on feedback, and weaving the change into the fabric of your team's culture, you can ensure that the changes you've implemented not only stick but also contribute to your team's long-term success and resilience.

STRATEGIES FOR CHANGE LEADERSHIP

Acknowledge That People Are Often Scared of Change: change can be unsettling, often pulling individuals away from their comfort zones and familiar territories. It's natural for people to feel apprehensive and resistant when faced with the unknown, especially considering the tumultuous events of recent years, such as those experienced in 2020 and 2021. Acknowledging and respecting these human emotions and the reluctance to embrace change is essential for facilitating progress. By empathising with individuals' concerns and offering support and guidance, leaders can help ease the transition and foster a more positive outlook towards change.

Explain What Happens When You Don't Change: When you resist change, you risk stagnation and falling behind in an ever-evolving world. While change may initially seem daunting, it's important to recognise that it also brings opportunities for growth and innovation. Without embracing change, your team and organisation can become stagnant, unable to adapt to shifting market dynamics or meet evolving customer needs.

Communicate, Communicate, Communicate: If you're going to initiate change you will need to explain things multiple times and to everyone, regardless of whether they are involved. This is because humans need information several times to move from knowing to understanding. We all need to feel involved to create a feeling of belonging that is critical to team dynamics. Do you know about the 'Rule of Seven'? Research tells us that repeating a message seven times is the optimal number of exposures needed to recall a message.

Create a Culture Where There Is No Fear of Failure: If possible, change things gradually and daily. If you encourage an environment of constant evolution and growth instead of a culture of perfection, when things go wrong, they won't feel as catastrophic. Small steps make it easy to undo a mistake. And we know that the tortoise always wins the race!

Never Berate Your Team for Making a Change That Doesn't Work, as long as the intention is to move forward. However, don't allow regressive change, as some people love to move backwards – don't tolerate that!

Encourage Change Even When It May Not Seem Necessary: Without a culture of change, we encourage 'learned helplessness' where we sit and wait for everyone else to help us because we feel we aren't allowed or don't know how to try things ourselves. Make change part of someone's goals or celebrate change initiatives, even if they fail!

Procrastination Is the Enemy of Success: Overthinking will kill change and progression. Don't allow your team to overthink... and wrap your arms around those that tend to. This is easier if changes are simple, small and regular. Make a decision and act immediately. Create a minimum viable product (MVP) or prototype and test it – but do something. Ideas don't create change, action does.

Impatience Is a Virtue: Impatience gets things done. Of course, impatience is not always a good thing, but it is vital to your success when it comes to change. While those around you are contemplating, you must act to stay ahead of the game. Give change to the drivers in your team, those who make things happen, the impatient ones. Then, spend time with the more reticent to nurture and support them. As Nike tells us, 'Just do it!'

Build Trust Through Transparency: Being open and honest is essential for building trust. Being transparent and communicating openly with your team about changes is essential. Arrange consistent meetings or check-ins to share updates on initiatives. Promote open communication, enable team members to ask questions and share their thoughts and allow time for the drivers to report back. Creating this open environment establishes the groundwork for team trust to grow.

Empower Team Members Through Ownership: Empowerment is essential to encouraging team members to take responsibility and own their work. Distribute authority so the team can make its own choices and feel pride in its work. Motivate them to plan out how they'll reach their objectives. Trust them to take charge of their projects and move them forward with your support and advice. One way to encourage independence and self-sufficiency in your team is to give them responsibility and authority.

Seek Feedback for Continuous Improvement: Feedback is essential for growth and improvement. Actively seek feedback from your team on your leadership style and the effectiveness of the change initiatives. Create opportunities for anonymous feedback through surveys or suggestion boxes to ensure everyone feels comfortable sharing their thoughts and ideas. Use this feedback to identify areas for improvement and implement changes accordingly. You demonstrate your commitment to learning and improvement as a leader by continuously seeking feedback.

Lead by Example: As a leader, your actions speak louder than words. In the face of change, set an example for others by exhibiting resilience, flexibility and positivity. Demonstrate to your team that you are dedicated to overcoming obstacles together and have faith in the organisation's vision and goals by demonstrating that you believe in them. Empathy and compassion are essential leadership qualities and you should make it a point to listen to the problems of your team members and offer assistance when required. To maintain a positive mood and keep the momentum rolling, it is important to celebrate accomplishments and milestones along the route.

Incorporating these actionable exercises and steps into your leadership style will enhance your ability to navigate team dynamics, especially amidst change. A successful change leader demonstrates patience, resilience and adaptability, fostering a culture of participation, transparency and continuous growth within the team. By engaging your team in this manner, you'll effectively guide them through challenging transitions, fostering resilience and intelligence in the process. Remember, those who embrace change emerge stronger and more capable, ready to tackle whatever lies ahead.

BRILLIANT TEAMS AND CHANGE LEADERSHIP

When it comes to change leadership, your brilliant team will:

- Effectively create opportunities in response to unanticipated changes.
- Effectively deal with each other's feelings and emotions when driving change.

- Understand that dealing with changing priorities is part of everyday work.
- Understand internal strengths and weaknesses through change.
- Understand external threats and opportunities for change.

KEY TAKEAWAYS

- **Transparency and Trust:** Building trust through transparent communication is essential for leading through change. Keeping your team informed and involved creates a sense of trust and confidence that will help you navigate even the most challenging transitions.
- **Empowerment and Ownership:** Empowering your team members by involving them in decision-making processes and giving them ownership of their work fosters a sense of accountability and commitment. When team members feel empowered, they are more likely to embrace and drive change.
- **Continuous Improvement:** Change is not a one-time event but a continuous process. Leaders must continually seek feedback, learn from successes and failures and adapt their approach accordingly. By embracing a continuous improvement mindset, leaders can more effectively navigate change and drive positive outcomes.
- **Leading by Example:** As a leader, you set the tone for how change is perceived and embraced within your organisation. Leading by example, demonstrating resilience, adaptability and a positive attitude inspires your team to follow suit. Your actions speak louder than words, so be intentional about the behaviours you model for your team.
- **Embracing Change Agent Role:** Leaders must embrace their role as change agents within their organisations.

Change is inevitable in today's fast-paced world, and leaders who can effectively navigate their teams through change will position their organisations for success. Embrace change as an opportunity for growth and innovation and lead your team confidently into the future.

5

DELIVERING OUTSTANDING RESULTS

'Results matter more than intentions. No matter how well-intentioned, if the results aren't there, it's not a success.'

— SUSAN WOJCICKI

F ostering a culture of camaraderie and mutual respect is undoubtedly valuable in our dynamic and competitive landscape. However, it's imperative to recognise that our ultimate goal extends beyond cultivating a great environment. You're here to drive growth and meet your customers' demands, as without fulfilling these objectives, your business cannot thrive.

Effective leaders must prioritise outcomes. Adopting a results-driven approach ensures that every action and resource is directed towards achieving strategic goals, ultimately leading to optimal performance and success. It's important to understand that our efforts' impact translates directly into the tangible results that propel our business forward.

Without a focus on delivering high-quality results, teams risk being inefficient and ineffective. Empowering your team to articulate their vision of success and effectiveness, particularly in terms of tangible results, is pivotal in assessing their current capabilities and future performance potential.

Teams may struggle to focus on results due to inherent self-interest and self-preservation instincts. Our natural inclination to prioritise personal interests, even within our teams and families, can spread rapidly, undermining teamwork and ultimately eroding trust. The key is prioritising the right objectives, ensuring distractions do not derail progress.

Good leaders recognise the significance of delivering exceptional results. Still, modern leadership moves beyond traditional ways of setting unattainable goals and pushing teams to the limit. With a staggering 79% of employees experiencing burnout[1], it's evident that striking a balance between high performance and well-being is paramount. This entails establishing realistic goals, crafting effective strategies and executing them responsibly. Leaders must prioritise continuous improvement and innovation to foster the team's sustainable growth.

Achieving brilliance requires leaders to do more than just analyse figures and acknowledge individual strengths. They must also grasp team dynamics and ensure that work fosters flow rather than stress. So, how can leaders strike this delicate balance?

UNDERSTANDING PEAK PERFORMANCE

In teamwork, peak performance occurs when a team operates at its highest level of efficiency and creativity, achieving outstanding results collaboratively. Peak performance is more than hard work and high effort; it involves harnessing each team member's strengths, seamless collaboration and deep engagement in tasks.

Psychologically, peak performance is intertwined with understanding each individual's personality types, team roles and

---

1. Spill. Feb 2024. Seventy workplace stress statistics you need to know in 2024.

preferences, and acknowledging each member's unique contributions.

For instance, some excel in creative brainstorming (reminiscent of Belbin's 'Plant' role), while others thrive in meticulous planning (as the 'Completer-Finisher'). This understanding enables tasks to align with natural inclinations and skills, fostering a state of 'flow'. Motivation also plays a crucial role, with external rewards being one aspect but internal drivers such as purpose, mastery and autonomy being equally significant. Clear goals are essential, too, providing direction and a sense of achievement as milestones are attained.

An enabling environment, where taking risks is encouraged and failures are embraced as opportunities for growth, forms the foundation for all of this. In such a setting, feedback is constructive and challenges are tackled with a mindset focused on growth. When these elements harmonise – from understanding personality types and setting clear goals to fostering a culture of support and ongoing learning – teams not only attain but can also sustain peak performance, flourishing even amidst adversity.

FOCUSING ON RESULTS: FOUR COMMON DISTRACTIONS

On the journey towards team success, you may encounter distractions that threaten to divert your focus from collective achievements. Ego emerges as a significant challenge. It subtly shifts the spotlight from 'we' to 'me', elevating individual success above the team's triumph. However, in cohesive teams, true joy is found not in individual accolades but in shared victories, necessitating a deliberate suppression of personal egos in favour of team glory.

Another distraction arises from career development and financial aspirations. Team members naturally aspire to personal growth and financial stability. Addressing these needs openly and without judgment is crucial, rooted in trust, which allows team members to express vulnerabilities without hindering the team's progress.

However, the most destructive distraction arises when the prioritisation of your reporting team or department overshadows your peer leadership team. It's tempting to feel a stronger allegiance to the team one leads, driven by duty and a fear of disappointment. Yet, this mindset can foster division rather than unity, with leaders advocating for their team interests instead of prioritising the organisation's best interests. True leadership success lies in prioritising the needs of the collective leadership team over individual departments, nurturing a familial environment where sacrifices are made for the greater good, with the ultimate reward being the success of the team as a whole. Your leadership peer group are your number one team!

UNDERSTANDING PERSONALITY TYPES

Imagine a team as a jigsaw puzzle. Each piece has its unique shape and place, contributing to the complete picture. This is how personality types work within a team, contributing to its peak performance. Inspired by Carl Jung's theories on extroversion and introversion, thinking and feeling, we can begin to understand how diverse personalities bring balance and depth to a team, enabling it to thrive.

What do I mean by this? Extroverts, with their energy and ease in social situations, often rally the team, share ideas openly and drive engagement. They're the spark in team discussions, bringing vibrancy to the workplace. On the other hand, introverts offer thoughtful insights and deep focus. They thrive in solitude, where they can process and develop innovative solutions. They ensure that the team's enthusiasm is balanced with depth and reflection.

Teams also have thinkers and feelers. Thinkers approach decisions with logic and objectivity, offering clarity and direction. They're crucial in navigating complex problems with a clear head. Feelers bring empathy and understanding, ensuring team cohesion and morale remain high. They're the glue that holds the team together during challenging times.

Understanding these dynamics allows leaders to craft a team where everyone plays to their strengths. Creating 'flow' – a state where work feels less like work and more like a natural extension of one's abilities – is proven to increase productivity and create happier and more fulfilled teams. This is where peak performance lives.

The leader's role is that of the conductor in an orchestra. They know who excels in creative brainstorming and who's better suited to meticulously managing projects. They recognise that introverts prefer diving deep into research rather than leading large meetings. At the same time, extroverts might thrive in building relationships rather than getting lost in spreadsheets.

In every team, there's a multitude of tasks that need completing. Have you ever disliked and put off tasks you don't want to do and then, to your amazement, you discover that someone in your team loves that exact task? It's a common scenario in great teams. They have a blend of team members who play to their strengths, enabling all tasks to be completed – even the boring ones – because, believe it or not, there's someone in your team who enjoys doing the repetitive, seemingly mundane tasks!

Creating a team that achieves peak performance requires embracing skill, thought and personality diversity. It's tempting for leaders to gravitate towards hiring mini versions of themselves (is this you?), but true strength lies in diversity. Every team needs a blend of extroverts and introverts, thinkers and feelers, each bringing unique perspectives and strengths.

Your job is to understand your team members deeply, not to mould them into something they're not, but to allow them to shine in their natural abilities. When you do this effectively, you won't just have a team that can execute tasks brilliantly but also one that innovates, adapts and thrives, regardless of its challenges.

When tasks aren't finished, the instinct may be to give it to the person who 'gets things done' to fill the gap. However, it's crucial to avoid forcing square pegs into round holes. Doing so risks bringing team members out of their 'zone of genius' and can lead to frustration and inefficiency. Instead, focus on bringing complementary pieces that enhance the team's overall capabilities. By filling the gaps strategically, you can ensure that each team member operates within their strengths and contributes effectively to the team's success.

Leaders seeking to better understand their team's personality types have various tools at their disposal. These tools help you to understand individual personalities and align tasks to each team member's strengths, promoting a thriving and efficient work environment.

One renowned framework is the Myers-Briggs Type Indicator (MBTI), which expands on Jung's theory of personality types. It categorises individuals into sixteen distinct personality types based on preferences like introversion vs. extroversion and thinking vs. feeling. Leaders can find MBTI assessments through certified practitioners or online platforms specialising in psychological assessments.

Another useful tool is the DiSC profile, which focuses on four primary behaviour types: Dominance, Influence, Steadiness and Conscientiousness. It offers insights into how team members prefer to work and interact, aiding leaders in fostering a harmonious and productive team dynamic. Information and access to DiSC assessments and the team workshops that we run are available through https://linktr.ee/bebrilliantconsultancy

By utilising the DiSC tool, you can gain valuable insights into your team's unique makeup. These insights empower you to create an environment where everyone can operate in their 'flow,' leveraging strengths for peak performance and improving communication and collaboration. The tool encourages diversity in thought and approach, ensuring a well-rounded and resilient team, capable of tackling any challenge.

PLAYING TO TEAM STRENGTHS

Finding your team's strengths is like discovering the secret ingredients that make your team uniquely brilliant. Beyond personality types, understanding each member's strengths can transform how your team works, creating an environment where everyone is in their element, contributing their best.

One of the most powerful tools for this dedicated exploration into strengths is the Gallup StrengthsFinder[2]. This assessment dives deep into the unique talents of each team member, identifying areas where they naturally excel and identifying an individual's top strengths from a list of thirty-four themes. Understanding each of your team member's top strengths helps you assign tasks that align with each person's natural abilities and preferences.

The beauty of Gallup's StrengthsFinder lies in its ability to highlight strengths that team members might not have been aware of. This opens up conversations about how these strengths can be leveraged, not just individually but within the team. It will help you better match tasks to those who will perform them well and enjoy doing them, boosting individual performance and elevating the entire team. You will be assured of better outcomes, higher satisfaction and outstanding results.

---

2. https://www.gallup.com/cliftonstrengths/en/254033/strengthsfinder

The Gallup StrengthsFinder can be accessed online, providing a straightforward way for individuals and teams to discover their strengths. It's an investment in your team's future, laying the foundation for a work environment where everyone is positioned to thrive.

MAINTAINING TEAM MOTIVATION

Maintaining team motivation is a perpetual challenge for leaders, especially during adversity or setbacks. Effectively keeping the team energised and moving forward, even in the face of challenges, hinges on understanding what drives your team and leveraging that insight to maintain high motivation levels.

First and foremost, autonomy plays a significant role. Granting your team the freedom to take ownership of tasks and make decisions fosters a sense of ownership and naturally fuels their desire to excel.

Equally important is task diversity. Introducing variety to assignments and responsibilities creates a dynamic and stimulating work environment, preventing monotony and disengagement. Leaders can achieve this by rotating tasks, offering cross-training opportunities or presenting new challenges that stretch team members' abilities.

Identity is closely linked to how much employees perceive the significance and impact of their work. Helping your team grasp the broader picture and illustrating how their efforts contribute to it fosters a deeper sense of purpose and motivation. You can reinforce this by clearly articulating the team's mission and vision, connecting the dots between daily tasks and overarching objectives.

Furthermore, the perceived impact of their work significantly influences motivation levels. When team members believe their contributions make a difference, motivation soars. It falls upon leaders to demonstrate how each individual's efforts contribute to the overall goals and celebrate their value.

Feedback is a vital tool for maintaining motivation and giving individuals a sense of progress and accomplishment. Regular, constructive feedback enables everyone to understand their performance, acknowledge achievements and identify areas for growth. You must prioritise offering timely and specific feedback, acknowledging successes and providing support when needed.

To keep motivation high, consider the following:

- Fostering a positive work culture built on trust, respect and collaboration.
- Celebrating big and small successes to recognise and reward achievements.
- Encouraging open communication and dialogue, allowing team members to voice their concerns and ideas.
- Providing opportunities for professional growth and development, investing in the skill enhancement of team members.
- Leading by example, demonstrating resilience, optimism and a commitment to excellence.

Despite challenges or setbacks, a motivated team is better equipped to overcome obstacles and drive success for the organisation as a whole.

RESULTS FROM RESILIENCE

Resilience is the muscle of your team's spirit; the stronger it is, the better it performs, especially during tough times. When teams can bounce back from failures and setbacks, adapt to change and push forward, even when obstacles seem insurmountable, performance follows. Resilience is intricately linked to performance as it equips your team to confront challenges head-on, extract valuable lessons from them and emerge stronger. By viewing every experience, whether positive or negative, as an opportunity for growth, your team cultivates a growth mindset that propels them towards their objectives.

Growth mindset and adaptability are key components of resilience – if you can view failures as opportunities to learn rather than insurmountable barriers, you foster long-term success by keeping your team open to learning and adapting, which is crucial in today's ever-changing environment.

We cover resilience in its chapter later in the book, still, it's important to understand how it contributes to peak performance and your team's wellbeing and culture. Later in the book, we'll explore strategies for fostering resilience, encouraging a growth mindset and enhancing adaptability, all aimed at equipping your team to thrive no matter what comes their way.

ACHIEVING CONSISTENCY IN RESULTS

Achieving consistent results is a complex challenge influenced by an ever-changing business environment, team diversity, resource limits, fluctuating motivation levels, inefficient processes and external pressures. The business world is always shifting, marked by continuous technological advancements and evolving market demands. Maintaining high performance requires agile adaptation and strategic alignment.

Each team member brings unique attributes and perspectives, necessitating thoughtful leadership to orchestrate productivity harmoniously. Strategic task prioritisation and management become imperative for optimal performance with limited resources. Sustaining motivation and engagement amidst fluctuating conditions is paramount, as shifts in dynamics can significantly impact team performance.

Outdated systems and processes can hinder reliable outcomes, and external factors such as economic fluctuations can further disrupt goal attainment. Addressing these challenges demands strategic planning, fostering a robust team culture, promoting ongoing learning and adaptation and effectively leveraging technology.

Consistency isn't just repeating the same steps; it's about building a culture where doing great work is just what the team does, fuelled by a united drive to excel.

LEADERSHIP STRATEGIES FOR PEAK PERFORMANCE

Clarity, routine and growth are pivotal pillars in achieving consistent results. Begin by delineating a clear vision of success, illustrating their integral role within the overarching objectives to your team. Standardising processes reduces ambiguity and enhances productivity by streamlining operations.

To maintain momentum, ensure your team remains sharp through regular training sessions, introducing innovative approaches to address recurrent challenges. Cultivate an environment where feedback is treasured, viewing mistakes as opportunities for growth and refinement. Additionally, implement robust metrics to gauge progress accurately – acknowledging and celebrating achievements is a potent motivator, instilling a sense of pride and purpose within the team.

SET CLEAR GOALS

We've already discussed the importance of setting goals in Chapter One. It really does make a big difference in getting great results and keeping the team motivated. Imagine a marketing leader setting a goal to 'increase website traffic'. This goal lacks a defined target to work towards and the ambiguity it creates can lead to disorganised efforts, inconsistent performance and demotivation among team members.

Now imagine the marketing leader setting a clear goal for their team – 'increase website traffic from our social media channels by 30% over the next quarter.' This goal is SMART: it's specific to website traffic from social media, measurable by the percentage increase, achievable with the right strategy, relevant to the broader aim of enhancing brand visibility and time-bound with a three-month deadline. The SMART goal provides clear direction, enabling the team to align their strategies, track progress effectively and focus on achieving tangible results. Plus, seeing progress towards this goal can rally the team, sparking their motivation and encouraging everyone to do their best to hit that target.

Setting clear, measurable goals gives your team direction and fuels their drive to achieve outstanding results. It provides a roadmap that aligns with our vision, encourages everyone to take ownership of their contributions and celebrates the milestones.

REVIEWING ORGANISATIONAL PERFORMANCE REGULARLY

Assessing your team's performance regularly is important to ensuring alignment and progress towards shared objectives. One effective method I employ is implementing a balanced scorecard approach.

The balanced scorecard offers a comprehensive view of performance across various dimensions beyond just financial metrics. While financial numbers are important, they only provide part of the picture. The balanced scorecard also considers factors like customer satisfaction, internal processes and team development.

Imagine your organisation as a plane on its flight path. While financial metrics are similar to monitoring speed and fuel levels, successful navigation requires a broader perspective. The balanced scorecard acts as your cockpit instrument panel, providing insights into the plane's condition, weather conditions and crew morale. With this comprehensive view, you can make informed decisions to ensure your team's smooth flight and direction towards its destination.

Financial Perspective: This is the traditional bottom-line view of performance, focusing on metrics like revenue, profitability and cost efficiency. But remember, numbers don't tell the whole story. Balancing financials with other factors ensures you're not just surviving but thriving long-term.

Customer Perspective: Happy customers are the lifeblood of any business. This perspective looks at customer satisfaction, loyalty and retention metrics. Understanding your customers' needs and preferences enables you to tailor your products and services to better meet their expectations, drive repeat purchases and drive loyalty.

Internal Processes are the behind-the-scenes operations that keep your business running smoothly. This perspective monitors how efficiently and effectively you're working behind the scenes. By continually optimising internal processes, you can reduce waste, improve productivity and enhance overall performance.

Learning and Growth: The ability to adapt and innovate is critical in today's rapidly changing business environment. This part of the scorecard examines how you're developing your team's skills and capabilities and fostering a culture that's ready for whatever comes next.

Regularly reviewing organisational performance using a balanced scorecard approach is essential for keeping everyone aligned with strategic goals and driving continuous improvement. By focusing on the four perspectives of financial, customer, internal processes and learning and growth, you can gain a holistic view of your organisation's performance and identify opportunities for optimisation. By establishing a structured review process and acting based on insights gathered, you can ensure that your team and organisation remain agile, resilient and well-positioned for future success.

To download a Balanced Scorecard template, visit:
https://linktr.ee/bebrilliantconsultancy

REGULAR INDIVIDUAL PERFORMANCE REVIEWS

Individual performance reviews are integral to achieving success. These one-on-one evaluations serve as valuable pauses amid the daily hustle, offering reflection, contemplation and adjustment opportunities. Whether an individual is riding high on a wave of accomplishments or grappling with challenges such as change or workload, these reviews play a pivotal role in fostering continuous improvement and nurturing personal connections within your team.

Regular performance reviews shed light on areas ripe for enhancement. Leaders can engage in candid discussions about prevailing challenges by meticulously analysing key metrics. By soliciting timely feedback from team members, leaders gain insights into areas where improvement is needed, enabling them to craft effective strategies for overcoming obstacles. Ultimately, these reviews empower individuals to surmount hurdles and reach new heights of success.

Continuous performance reviews are more than opportunities to identify areas for improvement. They also offer a platform to celebrate successes, regardless of their size. Recognising even the smallest accomplishments is a powerful incentive, uplifting morale, fostering a stronger work ethic and bolstering team unity.

Whether a project is completed on time, predetermined targets are exceeded, or exceptional customer service is delivered, acknowledging and applauding these achievements consistently encourages positive behaviours. Moreover, it cultivates a culture of appreciation and recognition within the team, further motivating individuals to strive for excellence.

But how do you conduct effective team performance reviews? Here are some guidelines to consider:

- **Prioritise Scheduled Meetings**: Schedule performance reviews in advance and prioritise them in both your and the individual's diaries. Avoid ad hoc meetings, as they can create anxiety and uncertainty. Planned meetings allow adequate preparation and ensure their occurrence.
- **Establish Clear Objectives:** Before embarking on a performance review, it is imperative to clearly define the purpose and objectives of the review meeting. Setting unambiguous objectives ensures all stakeholders are aligned and aware of the meeting's agenda.
- **Gather Pertinent Data:** Thoroughly gather data and feedback that offer insights into the individual's performance. This should include indicators such as KPIs, project milestones, customer feedback or ongoing behavioural observations. Armed with these insights, leaders can facilitate objective discussions and informed decision-making during the review process.
- **Cultivate a Supportive Environment:** Foster an atmosphere of trust and support where individuals feel comfortable sharing their thoughts, ideas and concerns without fear of repercussion. Encourage open and transparent communication and demonstrate receptiveness to constructive feedback.
- **Strike a Balance:** While it is vital to address areas requiring improvement, it is equally important to acknowledge and celebrate strengths and achievements. Strike a balance by highlighting successes and recognising

contributions while simultaneously delving into opportunities for growth and development.

- **Craft Actionable Plans:** Leverage the insights from the performance review to draft actionable improvement plans. Review SMART goals and help break down the necessary steps to achieve them. Assign responsibilities, establish timelines and track progress meticulously.
- **Sustain Momentum Through Follow-up and Monitoring:** A performance review should not be viewed as a standalone event but as part of an ongoing process. Follow up regularly to assess progress, reassess goals and make any requisite adjustments. By diligently monitoring progress, leaders ensure accountability and keep the team focused on continuous improvement.

Regular performance reviews are indispensable for identifying areas for enhancement, celebrating successes and nurturing a culture of continuous improvement within the team. Leaders can empower their teams to scale greater heights and unlock their full potential by fostering an environment conducive to open communication and growth.

LEARN FROM SHORTFALLS QUICKLY

Learning swiftly from triumphs and setbacks is paramount for a team's growth and advancement. By impartially scrutinising outcomes with data-driven insights and utilising your scorecard, you can evaluate the team's performance vis-a-vis established benchmarks, gaining a lucid comprehension of progress.

Reviewing your results and learning from successes and failures is vital for continuous improvement and team and organisation growth. Instead of solely relying on intuition or subjective evaluations, it is crucial to utilise quantitative and qualitative data to gauge performance, evaluating it against predefined metrics and benchmarks. This includes comprehensive assessments and a thorough review of KPIs. You must always validate the data, seeking the opinions of customers and important stakeholders to gain a better perception of outcomes than just numbers and data. For example, you may not have hit your metrics, but your customer experience was outstanding, driving longer-term loyalty.

When encountering obstacles or setbacks, avoid fixating on failures or pointing fingers and instead concentrate on grasping the underlying reasons and uncovering valuable insights. Negative feedback, shortcomings, or failures should be viewed as invaluable learning opportunities rather than impediments – use them to strengthen and evolve. Maintaining a positive perspective and regarding setbacks as opportunities for growth and development enables teams to glean vital lessons, refine their strategies and adeptly navigate challenges.

LEADERSHIP COMMUNICATION AND RESULTS

In Chapter Nine, we delve deeper into communication. However, it's crucial to acknowledge its pivotal role in achieving peak performance. Exceptional communication goes beyond information sharing; it inspires, unifies, and steers a team towards shared objectives. It is the bedrock for establishing clear expectations, providing valuable feedback and ensuring everyone remains aligned and motivated.

Effective communication is the linchpin for giving feedback, an indispensable ingredient for growth and enhancement. It highlights strengths and areas for improvement. It also acts as the heartbeat of motivation, inspiring teams and elucidating the value of their contributions, thus fostering a supportive atmosphere where everyone is compelled to deliver their best.

So, how can leaders effectively communicate to uphold a focus on results? They must adopt a clear, straightforward approach, minimising confusion and ensuring messages are easily understood. Equally significant is listening. Good leaders listen to and value their team's feedback, concerns and ideas, thereby nurturing trust and rapport. They tailor their communication methods to suit the message and audience, ensuring their messages resonate and are absorbed.

Ultimately, results-driven leadership is not just about achieving short-term goals; it's about cultivating a culture of excellence and driving sustainable success for your team and organisation. By embracing these principles and practices, you can unlock your team's full potential, foster collaboration and innovation and achieve remarkable results.

BRILLIANT TEAMS AND RESULTS

When it comes to delivering exceptional results, your brilliant team will:

- Have positive performance projections for the next year.
- Consistently deliver good results.
- Consistently meet their key performance indicators.
- Have a reputation for high performance.
- Perform to high standards on challenging projects.

KEY TAKEAWAYS

- **Balance High Performance With Well-being:** Modern leadership transcends old norms by setting achievable goals and executing plans carefully. This ensures the team's growth and avoids burnout. It also understands each team member's strengths, creating an environment where work feels natural and fostering continuous innovation.

- **Understand Your Team Members Better:** Peak performance involves recognising and utilising the team's diverse personality types and strengths. By aligning tasks with individual inclinations and fostering a supportive environment, teams can reach and sustain peak performance and thrive even in challenging times.

- **Leveraging Tools for Team Dynamics:** Tools like DiSC and Gallup's StrengthsFinder are invaluable for leaders to understand their team's unique makeup. This understanding enables leaders to align tasks with natural abilities, promoting efficiency, satisfaction and exceptional results.

- **Learn Quickly From Setbacks:** Building a resilient team with a growth mindset and adaptability is crucial for long-term success. Strategies for fostering resilience, enhancing adaptability and maintaining motivation are key to overcoming obstacles and achieving consistent results.

- **Strive For Consistency:** Achieving consistency in results requires setting clear goals, effective tracking and learning from successes and failures. Utilising the Balanced Scorecard helps align day-to-day efforts with strategic goals, fostering a culture of continuous improvement and teamwork essential for delivering outstanding results.

6

MEETING EFFECTIVENESS

'Meetings are places where the minutes are kept, and the hours are lost.'

— UNKNOWN

We are spending more and more time in meetings. On average, people spend nearly twenty-three hours a week in them, up from less than ten hours in the 1960s[1]. Moreover, the meetings are often poorly timed, badly run, or both. I am convinced that we all attend at least one meeting where we question the purpose and feel frustrated about the waste of our time as we leave. Meetings are a common problem in today's corporate world.

At their best, meetings can be efficient, dynamic and a great way to reach decisions, but at worst, they are places where ideas perish, egos dominate and a select few monopolise the conversation. Those who value participants' time, adhere diligently to agendas

---

1. Doodle. State of Meetings Report, 2019.

and encourage open communication are the ones most likely to yield tangible outcomes.

This is the harsh reality: poorly organised meetings come with repercussions; the economic and organisational toll of ineffective meetings is significant. A substantial amount of time and resources are squandered in unproductive meetings, highlighting the critical need to optimise meeting practices. When executed efficiently, meetings hold the promise of promoting inclusivity, stimulating innovation and bolstering Return on Investment (ROI). The solution is not to eliminate meetings entirely but to enhance their effectiveness. The key to success is emphasising quality over quantity.

However, it is not solely the responsibility of leaders. Individuals and teams must improve their meeting approach. Successful leaders quickly evaluate meeting effectiveness and recognise that each minute wasted in an inefficient meeting detracts from valuable work time.

Meetings can be a potent tool for driving change, promoting collaboration and achieving success. It's time to move away from unproductive meetings and welcome a new era of productivity and innovation.

WHY DO WE HAVE SO MANY MEETINGS?

The surge of meetings in the workplace often stems from a tangled array of factors. A trust deficit may lead leaders to closely monitor their teams, feeling the need for constant check-ins. Additionally, social loafing, where individuals contribute less in group settings and expect others to compensate, exacerbates the problem. Furthermore, the fear of missing out (FOMO) fuels a compulsion to participate in every discussion, lest something vital be overlooked.

Micromanagement exacerbates the situation, with leaders feeling compelled to oversee every detail, leading to excess coordination meetings. Additionally, unclear roles and responsibilities can create confusion, necessitating more meetings to determine who is doing what.

Decision-making paralysis, where uncertainty about who has the final say, results in meetings convened just to make decisions that could have been made independently. Remote and hybrid work models, while offering flexibility, introduce communication challenges, leading to more scheduled meetings as a substitute for informal office interactions.

Although digital communication tools are designed to streamline communication, they often result in a higher volume of meetings due to their ease of scheduling.

All these elements contribute to a culture where the default response to any issue or need for clarification is to schedule another meeting, despite the potential for more streamlined communication methods. Remember, when your team are in meetings, they are not doing anything else!

There's much advice on fixing meeting woes – set a clear agenda, stand up to keep it short or send someone else in your place – yet these fixes only scratch the surface. The real challenge lies deeper: meetings are intertwined with collaboration and individual productivity. And the irony? Despite the widespread dislike for them, those who complain about meetings often fiercely justify them as a 'necessary evil' for fostering collaboration, creativity and building relationships.

Executives, who aim to be team players, willingly bear the brunt, thinking they do what's best for the business. They ignore the broader impacts on the organisation's productivity, focus and morale. The hidden costs are immense, from squandered individual work time crucial for creativity to the disruption of 'deep work', pushing employees to find peace either early in the morning, late at night or over weekends... And we wonder why so many of our employees are burning out.

How employees view meeting effectiveness is closely tied to their job satisfaction. Rather than boosting communication and collaboration, ineffective meetings detract from these objectives, signalling a need for a fundamental shift in how meetings are perceived and conducted.

THE SILVER LINING

There's a positive side to all of this. By making meetings more effective, leaders can boost their team's productivity, engagement and ability to collaborate, leading to better outcomes all around. Establishing solid protocols is like laying the groundwork for a successful meeting. Without these guidelines, meetings can easily spiral into chaos, but with protocols, you can ensure that your meetings are purposeful and organised and that things get done. Here are some key steps to establish effective meeting protocols:

- **Define Clear Objectives**: Clearly articulate the meeting's purpose and desired outcomes to ensure alignment and focus among participants. This enables those invited to make an informed decision about whether to attend.
- **Develop Structured Agendas**: Think of the agenda as your roadmap for the meeting. It outlines what topics will be covered, what needs to be discussed and what outcomes you aim for. Sharing the agenda before the meeting allows everyone to come prepared and ready to dive right into the important stuff when the meeting starts. Create agendas that outline topics, timelines and responsibilities to guide discussions and maintain momentum.
- **Assign Roles and Responsibilities**: Every good meeting needs a leader, someone to keep things on track. You can

designate roles like a facilitator to guide the discussion, a timekeeper to ensure you stay on schedule and a note-taker to jot down key points. This way, everyone knows what they're responsible for and the meeting runs smoothly.

- **Encourage Active Participation**: A successful meeting is one in which everyone feels heard and valued. It is crucial to create an environment where people feel comfortable speaking up, sharing ideas and asking questions. Encouraging participation leads to better discussions and fosters a sense of ownership and teamwork. Rotate the roles between the team at each meeting.

- **Implement Decision-Making Processes**: Utilise consensus-building, voting or prioritisation techniques to facilitate effective decision-making and action planning.

- **Set Time Limits**: Time is precious, especially in meetings. Setting time limits for each agenda item keeps things moving and prevents discussions from dragging on endlessly. It also helps everyone stay focused and ensures you cover everything you need to in the time you have.

- **Follow-up and Accountability**: Once the meeting is over, it's important to follow up on any decisions. Assigning tasks and deadlines ensures that things get done and holds everyone accountable. It's all about ensuring the meeting isn't just a talk-fest but leads to tangible results.

- **Evaluate and Iterate**: Remember to step back and evaluate how the meeting went. Ask for feedback from participants and use it to improve future meetings. Maybe the agenda needs tweaking or the timing could be adjusted. By constantly refining your meeting protocols, you can ensure that your meetings always get better and more effective.

MAKING DECISIONS

Facilitating decision-making is paramount for effective meetings. Amidst the complexity, making decisions can often feel like navigating a maze. However, it doesn't need to be daunting. You can streamline this process with the right approach, leading to clear outcomes that drive your team's progress. Guiding your team from discussion to concrete decisions distinguishes productive meetings from aimless ones. Here are some strategies to ensure that decision-making is efficient, inclusive and ultimately effective:

- **Clarify Objectives**: Before discussing anything, it's crucial to clarify the meeting's objectives. What decision needs to be made? What problem are you trying to solve? By clearly defining the purpose of the meeting, you can keep discussions focused and avoid getting side-tracked.
- **Invite Relevant Stakeholders**: Decision-making is most effective when all relevant stakeholders are involved. Ensure that key team members or stakeholders with relevant expertise or input on the decision are invited. Their perspectives can provide valuable insights and help ensure that decisions are well-informed and inclusive. If they can't attend the meeting, get their position and ask their permission to represent them at the meeting so decisions aren't slowed down.
- **Generate Options:** Encourage brainstorming and idea generation to explore different options or solutions. Create a safe space for team members to share their thoughts and opinions. The goal is to generate a range of options to consider before deciding.
- **Evaluate Alternatives:** After generating options, it's time to evaluate their pros and cons. Consider factors such as feasibility, impact and alignment with organisational goals. Discuss each option's potential risks and benefits to make an informed decision.

- **Seek Consensus:** Aim to reach a consensus among team members whenever possible. Encourage open dialogue and constructive debate to address any concerns or reservations. By seeking consensus, you ensure everyone is on board with the decision and committed to its implementation.
- **Summarise Decisions:** At the end of the meeting, take a moment to summarise the decisions. Clarify what actions need to be taken and by whom. This ensures everyone is on the same page and understands their responsibilities.
- **Assign the Next Steps**: Assign specific next steps to individuals or teams to ensure accountability and follow-through. Clearly define deadlines and expectations for each action item. Assigning the next steps helps prevent tasks from falling through the cracks and keeps progress on track.
- **Document Decisions**: Documenting decisions is essential to ensuring accountability and providing a reference point for future meetings. Keep meeting minutes or notes that capture key decisions, the following steps and responsible parties. This documentation serves as a valuable resource for tracking progress and ensuring continuity.
- **Allow Sufficient Time for the Discussion!**

These steps help facilitate effective decision-making during meetings and clarify the next steps. Clear decisions and actionable next steps are the foundation for driving progress and achieving success as a team.

SETTING UP AN ANNUAL MEETING CYCLE

In Patrick Lencioni's 'The Five Dysfunctions of a Team' model[2], he delves into the structure and execution of meetings within an

---

2. Patrick Lencioni. The Five Dysfunctions of a Team.

organisation, emphasising their role in fostering positive team dynamics and overall effectiveness. Implementing a regular meeting cycle, which includes annual strategic planning, quarterly reviews, monthly team performance assessments and weekly tactical activity reviews, can profoundly improve a team's functionality and unity.

Annual Strategic Planning (Two Days): By dedicating two days annually to strategic planning, teams can openly discuss their visions, goals and challenges for the year ahead. This level of deep, strategic conversation fosters an environment where vulnerabilities can be shared – a foundational element of trust.

Quarterly Reviews (Half a Day): Quarterly reviews address potential conflict and commitment issues. Spending half a day reviewing progress towards strategic goals every three months allows team members to engage in healthy debates about directions and adjustments needed, fostering a culture of constructive conflict. It also reinforces commitment to the agreed-upon strategic objectives as team members collectively review and adjust their plans.

Monthly Team Performance Reviews (Two Hours): Monthly reviews are crucial for accountability. In these two-hour sessions, the team assesses their performance against the objectives and holds each other accountable for their contributions. This regular cadence ensures that accountability becomes a norm within the team's culture.

Weekly One-Two Hour Tactical Activity Reviews: Weekly meetings should focus on results. These sessions allow teams to stay aligned on immediate tasks and projects, ensuring that everyone contributes effectively to the team's short-term goals and, ultimately, the long-term strategic vision.

SEPARATING TACTICAL FROM STRATEGIC MEETINGS

Meetings are essential in business, functioning like the gears that maintain operational efficiency. Like a well-oiled machine, which needs different types of gear for various functions, an organisation requires a variety of meetings to achieve its goals effectively. This is where the idea of distinguishing tactical from strategic meetings becomes relevant.

Tactical meetings are essential for the smooth functioning of daily operations. They focus on addressing immediate challenges, solving problems and making decisions to ensure smooth operations. These meetings are usually brief, action-focused and include all team members. Examples of tactical meetings include daily stand-ups, project status updates and problem-solving sessions. They need to be held weekly.

Strategic meetings are the compass that directs the ship towards its long-term destination. They focus on strategic thinking, establishing long-term objectives and making key decisions influencing the organisation's future trajectory. Typically, these meetings are lengthier, more focused on strategy and include senior leadership and key stakeholders. Strategic meetings may include annual planning sessions, quarterly business reviews and executive strategy retreats.

The key to success is maintaining a clear distinction between the two, ensuring that each meeting's purpose is understood and respected. This separation allows for more focused discussions, optimal use of time and resources and the involvement of the right people in the right conversations.

Meeting leads should rigorously enforce this distinction, keeping discussions on track to ensure that tactical meetings address immediate issues. In contrast, strategic meetings focus on broader, future-oriented planning. This disciplined approach enhances decision-making and ensures that day-to-day tasks and long-term strategic objectives are pursued equally.

To access my Meeting Effectiveness Toolkit, including all the resources you need to improve your meetings, visit:

https://linktr.ee/bebrilliantconsultancy

BRILLIANT TEAMS AND MEETINGS

When it comes to delivering effective meetings, your brilliant team will:

- Have established protocols in place to ensure meetings are managed efficiently.
- Finish team meetings with clear decisions and next steps.
- Have a meeting cycle in place for the year.
- Review organisational performance against strategy regularly.
- Separate tactical from strategic meetings.

KEY TAKEAWAYS

- **Emphasise meeting quality** over quantity to enhance effectiveness, inclusivity and ROI.
- **Address the root causes of excessive meetings**, including lack of trust, fear of missing out and unclear roles, to reduce unnecessary gatherings.
- **Implement structured meeting protocols**, like setting clear objectives and roles, to ensure purposeful meetings lead to actionable outcomes.
- **Distinguish between tactical and strategic meetings** to maintain focus and effectively use time, ensuring each serves its specific purpose without overlap.

- **Establish a clear annual meeting cycle**, including strategic planning and regular reviews, to foster a culture of continuous improvement and alignment with organisational goals.

SECTION III

CULTURE: THE ART OF BRILLIANT TEAMS

Team culture is the beating heart of any organisation. It's the unseen force shaping behaviour, the shared values, beliefs and norms dictating how a team interacts, solves problems and achieves its goals. In brilliant teams, culture is not left to chance – it's deliberately cultivated, guided and connected to every facet of the team's operations.

Leaders play a key role in shaping the team culture through their actions, decisions and values. Implementing compassionate leadership can significantly impact team dynamics and morale. Great leadership is about setting a great example and embodying the behaviours and values you want to see in your team to create a strong culture. Culture can be defined as:

A Bedrock of Excellence: A strong, positive culture acts as the bedrock upon which the pillars of brilliance are built. It creates an environment where excellence is not just expected but inherently woven into the team's identity. When team members share a common culture, they are united by a collective pursuit of excellence that goes beyond individual aspirations and leads to extraordinary achievements.

The Catalyst for Engagement and Retention: Culture is the catalyst that drives engagement and retention. Teams with a vibrant and positive culture attract talent and retain it. Members of such teams are more likely to be committed to their work, feel a sense of belonging, and be motivated to go above and beyond in their roles, not because they must, but because they want to.

The Enabler of Adaptation and Change Culture: Exceptional teams demonstrate agility and resilience in facing challenges. A culture that welcomes and facilitates change prioritises learning, and fosters innovation is indispensable for enabling teams to adapt promptly and efficiently to new circumstances.

The Glue of Trust and Collaboration: Trust is at the heart of a high-performance culture. Trust fosters open communication, reduces friction and enables seamless collaboration. It is the glue that holds the team together, especially when faced with challenges. Where there is trust, there is a willingness to share ideas freely, challenge one another respectfully and work towards a common goal with shared vigour.

The Compass for Decision-Making: Culture acts as a compass for decision-making, guiding the team consistently in the right direction. When faced with difficult choices, a strong culture provides a reference point that helps team members make decisions that are in alignment with the team's values and objectives.

A Strong Team Culture is an Anchor in Times of Turbulence: A strong team culture provides stability and a sense of continuity that helps team members stay focused and productive even when external conditions are uncertain.

TOXIC CULTURES

As you build and lead exceptional teams, you must confront one of the greatest obstacles to success: a toxic culture. This environment, steeped in negativity, casts long shadows over every aspect of an organisation, undermining the very essence of teamwork and achievement.

A toxic culture manifests in various harmful ways. First, it takes a toll on your team members' well-being, fuelling stress and burnout and diminishing their engagement and passion for their work. This erosion of well-being directly impacts your team's fabric, fraying the bonds of trust and morale. In such an atmosphere, fear replaces confidence, suspicion overshadows trust and the vibrant energy that drives our teams forward begins to wane.

The implications extend beyond the internal dynamics of our teams. A toxic culture leads to a revolving door of talent, with high turnover rates signalling a deeper issue of disengagement and dissatisfaction. The cost is not just the resources spent on recruitment and training but also the loss of the collective wisdom and spirit that define your organisation.

Your ability to innovate and stay competitive is equally compromised. In a climate where fear stifles creativity, your edge in the marketplace dulls, leaving you trailing behind those who cultivate environments where ideas flourish. Additionally, the external perception of your organisation suffers, making it challenging to attract new talent and maintain healthy relationships with partners and customers.

At the root of many toxic cultures is leadership that fails to address or, worse, contributes to the negativity. This leadership breakdown affects the immediate team environment and exposes the organisation to legal and financial risks. Personal conflicts become pervasive, detracting from collaboration and cohesion and impairing your teams' effectiveness.

Yet, this challenge presents a profound opportunity for transformation. Tackling a toxic culture demands more than surface-level fixes; it requires a foundational shift towards trust, respect and support. Leaders must embody empathy, integrity and accountability, fostering an environment where open communication, positive behaviours and the well-being of every team member are paramount.

Transitioning from a toxic culture to one characterised by resilience and innovation is undoubtedly a daunting journey, yet it holds the promise of remarkable outcomes. Acknowledging existing challenges while fully embracing the imperative for transformation demands acknowledging values such as respect, collaboration and shared success. Emphasising such values paves the way for rebuilding your organisation upon a bedrock of vitality, health and sustained prosperity. Though the road may be arduous, steadfast commitment to this path can yield exceptional results, fostering a culture that thrives despite adversity.

THE IMPACT OF A TOXIC CULTURE

Teams with high levels of engagement enjoy a significant 43% reduction in employee turnover compared to less engaged teams. Conversely, employees who feel disconnected from their organisation's culture are 24% more inclined to explore other opportunities[1] – a substantial impact of disengagement. Beyond talent loss, this disengagement is costing companies billions – in the US alone, the figure stands at $550bn a year.[2]

Companies with highly engaged employees not only retain their teams but also generate a remarkable 18% increase in revenue and 23% greater profitability. A thriving culture elevates employee

---

1. Gallup. Employee Engagement vs. Employee Satisfaction and Organizational Culture.
2. Gallup. How to Tackle U.S. Employees' Stagnating Engagement.

satisfaction rates by up to 80% and substantially enhances the likelihood of revenue growth by over 400%.[3]

Furthermore, in today's business landscape, characterised by frequent mergers and acquisitions, 95% of executives describe cultural fit as critical to the integration's success.[4] This emphasises the importance of cultural compatibility and organisational harmony for the success of such endeavours. Amid these success stories of engagement and cultural synergy, a cautionary tale exists: actively disengaged employees can undermine organisational productivity.

The chapters ahead will help you pave the way to a happy, vibrant, collaborative and communicative culture.

WORKFORCE CHALLENGES

The modern workplace is a diverse blend of generations, each contributing unique perspectives, skills and communication styles. Multigenerational teams and the whirlwind of digital transformation present unique challenges and opportunities. While multigenerational teams offer numerous advantages, fostering a cohesive culture amidst such diversity can pose challenges. Therefore, leaders must strategise how to navigate these complexities effectively, harnessing the full potential of diversity within their teams to cultivate an inclusive and unified environment.

The presence of Traditionalists to Generation Z in a single team enriches the fabric of collaboration with diverse experiences and viewpoints. However, it also introduces complexities such as variations in communication styles, expectations regarding work-life balance and levels of technological adaptability. While these

---

3. Forbes. Does corporate culture drive financial performance?
4. McKinsey. March 2019. Organisational culture in mergers. Addressing the unseen forces.

differences can stimulate innovative solutions, they may also result in misunderstandings if not managed carefully.

Amid digital transformation, collaboration and communication have profoundly changed, demanding adaptability and a steadfast commitment to continuous learning from all team members. While this era of technological advancement enhances collaboration and presents new avenues to maintain team cohesion, even in remote or hybrid setups, it also poses challenges in preserving a strong team culture.

This book acknowledges these multifaceted challenges but does not delve deeply into multigenerational teams or digital transformation. Instead, it provides practical strategies and insights to navigate these complexities. Leaders can leverage the strengths of a diverse team by fostering open dialogue, customising leadership approaches and promoting inclusivity and mentorship.

7

THE TRUST EQUATION

'The best way to find out if you can trust somebody is to trust them.'

— ERNEST HEMINGWAY

Trust is the invisible glue that holds teams together, driving collaboration, cohesion and success. It's the cornerstone upon which relationships are built and productivity flourishes.

The significance of trust cannot be overstated. Anyone with experience working with teammates or leaders they don't trust will understand that trust is essential for effective collaboration and leadership. How can you fully commit to a shared goal if you have doubts about others' intentions or abilities? Trust demands vulnerability; it necessitates being open to others' behaviours, with the positive belief that they will act in alignment with expectations and demonstrate trustworthiness.

Imagine being part of a team where trust is abundant. It feels good, doesn't it? Members feel safe to voice their opinions, share their ideas, and take calculated risks without fear of judgment or reprisal. Conflicts are resolved swiftly in such an environment and creativity thrives as individuals feel empowered to contribute their unique perspectives to collective endeavours.

Conversely, in an atmosphere of distrust, teamwork falters and conflicts escalate, hindering progress and stifling innovation. Without trust, communication breaks down, collaboration becomes strained and performance suffers as individuals focus more on self-preservation than collective success.

Trust is the foundation for effective teamwork. It shapes the dynamics of task accomplishment and cultivates a climate of psychological safety and mutual encouragement among team members. When trust is ingrained in the team culture, individuals are emboldened to collaborate, explore innovative solutions and challenge conventional norms, ultimately resulting in elevated performance and the attainment of objectives.

Trust is more than just a nice idea – it's a tangible quality that can be cultivated and strengthened over time. By prioritising the development of trust and creating an atmosphere of openness, transparency and respect, you lay the groundwork for teams to thrive in today's dynamic and intricate work environments.

THE ROLE OF TRUST IN TEAM DYNAMICS

Communication is the lifeblood of a successful team, and trust acts as its catalyst. When team members trust one another, they are inclined to communicate openly, honestly and transparently. They feel secure in expressing their thoughts, ideas and concerns without fear of judgment or reprisal. This open communication fosters clarity, alignment and understanding, laying the groundwork for effective collaboration and problem-solving. But what does trust within a team entail? Trust within a team can be broken down into three key components:

Competence: The belief that team members can perform their tasks effectively and be relied upon to deliver results.

Benevolence: The assurance that team members will act in the team's best interests, prioritising the collective needs over personal ego or agendas.

Integrity: Behaving in alignment with established principles and values and being trusted to follow through on team commitments.

When trust is present, individuals feel comfortable assigning tasks, sharing responsibilities and tapping into each other's expertise. They know their intentions and capabilities will be respected, so they are more inclined to cooperate, innovate and explore new ideas, increasing creativity and productivity.

Trust levels within the team significantly impact overall performance. A culture of trust fosters accountability, where team members take ownership of their actions, uphold their commitments and strive for excellence. This sense of accountability motivates individuals to deliver their best work, confident that their peers value and respect their contributions. Consequently, teams with high trust consistently achieve better results, meet deadlines more reliably and adapt more effectively to changes in their environment.

One of the most renowned books on teamwork, Patrick Lencioni's The Five Dysfunctions of a Team, unequivocally states that 'Without trust, teamwork is impossible.' Lencioni delves into the critical role of trust in fostering effective team dynamics, emphasising the need for a culture where members feel safe being vulnerable and expressing their true selves. Without trust as a foundation, teams struggle to cultivate open communication, collaboration and mutual support, ultimately impeding their ability to perform at their best.

Team members don't always find it easy to share their thoughts, concerns or ideas, underscoring the importance of enhancing mutual support among colleagues. Establishing trust can be challenging, especially with individuals outside one's immediate circle. Yet, it's disheartening to witness team members engage in negative behaviour instead of collaborating and fostering unity.

In the workplace, we frequently rely on our colleagues to handle critical tasks such as drafting reports, managing client communications or finding solutions to challenges. Teams thrive when there's mutual trust that individuals will fulfil their responsibilities and excel in their roles.

Building trust hinges on establishing strong relationships. Understanding one another deeply is paramount before placing trust in each other. By demonstrating genuine interest in both the personal and professional lives of others, we can make them feel valued and motivated to reciprocate. It's fascinating how mutual respect and appreciation naturally bring individuals together.

Interestingly, many leaders prioritise their growth over that of their team members. Fostering trust and open communication is difficult without thoroughly understanding the team's capabilities. Leaders who prioritise trust-building and empowerment overexerting control and giving orders can achieve more significant outcomes, boost team morale and drive overall team performance.

PSYCHOLOGICAL SAFETY

Research on the relationship between team trust and performance has yielded conflicting findings, leading to puzzling conclusions. While some studies suggest that higher levels of trust do not necessarily translate to better team performance, others point to trust as a significant factor. However, recent insights from Google's Project Aristotle shed light on a critical aspect that surpasses mere trust: psychological safety.[1]

---

1. Google. Project Aristotle Report.

Project Aristotle, a two-year endeavour by Google analysing the behaviour of 180 teams across various functions, aimed to uncover what set their highest-performing teams apart. Surprisingly, the study found that psychological safety emerged as the most crucial factor. Teams with the highest levels of psychological safety outperformed their counterparts by an impressive 17%, while those with the lowest levels underperformed by 19%.

Psychological safety, essentially the feeling of being able to take risks without fear of judgment or repercussions, is a fundamental aspect of trust within a team. In psychologically safe environments, team members feel comfortable sharing their ideas, challenging existing notions and admitting mistakes without feeling insecure or embarrassed. Conversely, in teams lacking psychological safety, individuals hesitate to voice their opinions or hold others accountable, hindering team performance.

Google's findings introduced the importance of cultivating psychological safety within teams. Teams with high psychological safety were less likely to experience employee resignations and tended to generate more revenue and be rated as more effective by executives twice as often as their counterparts. This highlights the profound impact of psychological safety on team cohesion, innovation and overall performance, surpassing the traditional understanding of trust alone.

BUILDING TRUST WITHIN TEAMS

Establishing trust within a team requires time, effort and consistent nurturing. Trust is comparable to a delicate plant that needs open communication to be nourished, transparency to allow sunlight to penetrate and consistency to flourish.

As the saying goes, 'Trust takes years to build, seconds to break and forever to repair.' It evolves gradually through a series of events and interactions in which dependability, integrity and genuine concern for team members' wellbeing are consistently demonstrated. However, broken promises, dishonesty or inconsistency can quickly erode trust.

Building trust should be viewed as a long-term investment rather than a quick fix. Leaders can prioritise trust-building efforts by fostering a culture of openness, transparency and respect. So, what are the most effective strategies for establishing trust within a team as a leader?

VULNERABILITY-BASED TRUST

Building vulnerability-based trust within a team hinges on honesty and authenticity. As a leader, it's essential to have the courage to reveal your true self, including your strengths, weaknesses, fears and insecurities. By doing so, you develop stronger connections and relationships within the team.

This journey starts with self-awareness and acceptance of your own imperfections. Recognise that you don't have all the answers and be open to input and feedback from others. Embrace vulnerability as a sign of authenticity and humility rather than weakness. By demonstrating vulnerability, you inspire trust and respect among team members.

Leading by example, you create an environment where team members feel safe to be themselves and share their thoughts and concerns without fear of judgment. When team members trust each other enough to show vulnerability, they are more inclined to collaborate openly, communicate effectively and support one another through challenges. This fosters a culture of psychological safety, leading to increased team creativity, innovation and resilience.

Here are some questions or statements you can use:

'I appreciate honesty and openness in our team. What can I do to make you feel more comfortable sharing your thoughts and concerns?'

This statement communicates your commitment to creating a safe space for vulnerability and invites team members to share any barriers to being authentic.

'Here's a challenge I faced recently and how I overcame it. Tell me about your experiences as well.'

By sharing your own vulnerabilities and challenges, you set the tone for openness and encourage others to do the same.

'I'd like to have a culture where we can learn and grow together. I encourage everyone to share both successes and failures, as they are valuable learning experiences.'

This statement emphasises the importance of learning from both successes and failures and encourages team members to embrace vulnerability in their interactions.

SHARE EXPERIENCES

One effective way to cultivate vulnerability within your team is to share your own personal stories and experiences while also encouraging team members to do the same. These stories can encompass moments of failure, setbacks or instances of self-doubt and the strategies employed to overcome them. By openly sharing vulnerabilities, you convey that making mistakes is natural and that failure is integral to the learning journey.

Sharing personal experiences builds empathy, understanding and camaraderie among team members. It enables individuals to recognise the shared humanity and common purpose underpinning their collective efforts, strengthening their interpersonal connections. It allows team members to appreciate each other as individuals with unique backgrounds, perspectives and challenges.

Through sharing personal stories, teams can break down silos and promote cross-functional collaboration. By learning from one another's experiences and expertise, team members can enhance their problem-solving abilities and drive innovation.

However, it's crucial to strike a balance when sharing personal stories, ensuring that the level of disclosure remains appropriate for the professional setting. While opening up about life experiences can humanise leaders and foster stronger connections, oversharing or delving into overly personal details may make others uncomfortable. It's essential to share enough to demonstrate authenticity and relatability while respecting everyone's comfort levels and maintaining professional boundaries.

ADMIT MISTAKES

Mistakes are inevitable within teams, yet openly admitting them can prove challenging. However, far from being a sign of weakness, admitting mistakes demonstrates integrity, accountability and humility. When team members embrace a culture where mistakes are acknowledged openly, it fosters an environment of mutual respect and understanding.

By openly admitting mistakes, team members communicate that vulnerability is accepted and valued within the team dynamic. This openness encourages others to follow suit, contributing to a culture where honesty and authenticity are cherished qualities. Admitting mistakes creates valuable learning opportunities, as team members can collectively analyse what went wrong, brainstorm solutions and ultimately emerge stronger as a cohesive unit.

Openly admitting mistakes humanises leaders and team members, breaks down barriers and fosters deeper connections among individuals. It reinforces the notion that everyone is fallible and that pursuing excellence involves embracing setbacks as opportunities for growth and improvement.

SEEK FEEDBACK AND ASK FOR HELP

Seeking feedback and asking for help are powerful actions that demonstrate vulnerability and cultivate trust within a team. When leaders openly solicit feedback on aspects such as their leadership style, decision-making process or communication methods, they profoundly respect their team's perspectives and nurture a culture founded on collaboration and mutual respect. Similarly, acknowledging that you don't possess all the answers and being willing to seek assistance when necessary – whether from a mentor, the team or in confronting challenges – exemplifies humility and vulnerability.

However, it's crucial to approach this authentically. Some leaders may overdo this, feigning ignorance to elicit feedback, which can ultimately undermine trust. Authenticity is key; only seek feedback when genuinely warranted. If you truly lack the answers, view it as an opportunity to showcase your commitment to continual learning and growth. It's about striking a balance: being transparent about your limitations while avoiding the temptation to fabricate situations solely to deepen connections.

BE CONSISTENT

Consistency over time leads to trust. Those who consistently demonstrate reliable actions, make predictable decisions and communicate clearly create an environment of stability that comforts those around them. Consider the unsettling feeling of uncertainty when the ground beneath you constantly shifts – trust begins to erode.

In contrast, consistency provides a solid foundation. It means team members know what to expect, can trust their leader's word and feel secure in their working environment. Over time, this reliability fosters deep trust, as individuals feel valued and understood within a steadfast framework. When leaders demonstrate consistency, they send a resounding message: 'You can rely on me, regardless of the circumstances.' This sense of assurance is pivotal for nurturing an atmosphere where trust flourishes.

BE TRANSPARENT

Leaders can cultivate an environment that naturally fosters trust by prioritising transparency, open communication, empathy and empowerment. Transparency goes beyond sharing - when you openly discuss challenges, decisions and uncertainties, you're not just informing everyone but inviting them into the conversation. This transparent approach demonstrates respect and trust in the team's ability to handle the truth, encouraging reciprocal openness and honesty.

By prioritising transparency, you emphasise the importance of integrity and openness. These values are essential for creating a safe and inclusive space where team members feel valued and empowered to voice their thoughts, share ideas and contribute fully. Transparency sets the tone for how the team operates, making it clear that honesty is valued above all else and that every team member's perspective is valuable and respected.

CREATE A CULTURE OF BELONGING

Brené Brown, a prominent researcher on vulnerability and connection, indicated the significance of belonging and its deep connection to creating deeper trust. She distinguished between fitting in and belonging, asserting that true belonging doesn't require us to change WHO we are but to BE who we are. Belonging is the innate human desire to be part of something larger than ourselves. Because this longing is so fundamental, we often attempt to attain it by fitting in and seeking approval, actions that can undermine trust and result in disconnection.

Brown argues that for a team to foster a sense of belonging, its members and leaders must embrace vulnerability, practice empathy and cultivate a culture of authenticity and inclusiveness. Trust thrives within this space – where individuals feel seen, heard and valued. Trust rooted in belonging is potent because it fosters collaboration, innovation and resilience in the face of challenges, serving as the foundation for the team's ability to achieve remarkable results together.

Feeling connected and part of something greater than ourselves addresses one of our most fundamental human needs. When team members feel they belong, they are more inclined to trust their leaders and one another.

HAVE ZERO TOLERANCE OF GOSSIP

Despite its possible benign intentions, gossip can have a detrimental impact on team dynamics, morale and overall wellbeing. You must develop an antenna that instantly recognises gossip and treats it as the nemesis of team vitality.

So, how do you handle gossip in your team? Have you experienced the negative effects of gossip first-hand? Perhaps you felt unsettled, frustrated or even betrayed by those who gossiped. Gossip erodes trust among team members, creating a toxic environment where individuals feel uneasy and unsupported.

When gossip permeates a team, it damages relationships and undermines productivity and collaboration. Rumours and speculation can lead to misunderstandings, resentment and a breakdown in communication. They breed negativity, sowing seeds of discord and discontent within the team.

You must set clear expectations and communicate unequivocally that gossip will not be tolerated. Encourage open and direct communication so that team members feel empowered to address concerns or conflicts constructively.

CREATING GENUINE CONNECTIONS: BUILDING RELATIONSHIPS

Our working week can often feel like a whirlwind, where tasks pile up and meetings fill our calendars, so it's easy to forget the profound importance of forming genuine relationships in the workplace.

It starts subtly. You may miss team outings due to looming deadlines or underestimate the significance of casual conversations or coffee breaks with colleagues. Before you know it, you've inadvertently distanced yourself from your team, colleagues and even clients.

The impact might seem minor at first, but it doesn't take long for it to become apparent. There's a noticeable lack of cohesion within your team, leading to communication breakdown and a palpable decrease in morale. Projects begin to suffer, and the once vibrant office environment feels stagnant and disconnected.

Opportunities for collaboration and growth slip away outside the office. Networking events pass by unnoticed and potential partnerships fade into obscurity. Without authentic connections, your professional network stagnates, leaving you isolated amid a sea of missed opportunities.

But there's a solution. By investing time and effort into nurturing authentic connections, you can breathe new life into your team, ignite collaboration and unlock a world of possibilities beyond the confines of your office. Building relationships among team members is essential for fostering a united and cooperative atmosphere. Strong relationships breed camaraderie and trust, laying the groundwork for improved teamwork, communication and problem-solving.

Engage in regular social activities or team-building exercises. Whether it's a casual lunch outing, a team picnic or a workshop, these activities provide valuable opportunities for team members to bond, unwind and forge personal connections. Sharing personal stories outside work can deepen these bonds, strengthen trust and enhance relationships.

Collaborate on shared projects. Working together towards a common goal promotes solidarity and direction, ultimately building trust. Collaborative projects allow team members to leverage each other's strengths, learn from one another and achieve greater success together.

Trust is at the heart of team cohesiveness and is nurtured through genuine care, understanding and the freedom for each member to express their authentic selves. As you cultivate this environment of trust and support, your team will be more inclined to prioritise collective objectives over personal agendas. Small acts of kindness and genuine appreciation weave a tight-knit fabric of trust and loyalty within the team.

The essential elements of creativity, collaboration and innovation flourish in this fertile ground of trust. Individuals come together, united by shared goals and mutual respect, propelled by the strength of their collective trust and support. Trust isn't just a component of team dynamics; it's the very essence that binds individuals into a unified force where the common goal reigns supreme.

BRILLIANT TEAMS AND TRUST

When it comes to trust, your brilliant team will:

- Admit when they make mistakes.
- Have a high level of trust in each other's competency.
- Build trust by openly sharing their personal work experiences.
- Care about each other.
- Have a strong sense of connection with one another.

KEY TAKEAWAYS

- **Trust is the bedrock of successful teamwork and productivity,** emphasising the importance of cultivating an environment where team members feel secure, respected and valued.
- **Fostering vulnerability-based trust** involves embracing authenticity and openness within the team. This means encouraging team members to express their thoughts, feelings and concerns without fear of judgment, fostering a culture of transparency and genuine connection.
- **Admitting mistakes and sharing experiences** are powerful mechanisms for building team trust. When leaders and team members openly acknowledge their imperfections and share their experiences, it fosters a culture of honesty, accountability and mutual respect. This openness allows team members to learn from each other's experiences and work collaboratively toward shared goals.
- **Caring for each other** goes beyond professional relationships; it involves showing empathy, compassion and support. When team members feel genuinely cared for and valued, they feel a sense of camaraderie and

belonging, strengthening team cohesion and morale. This sense of connection fosters a collaborative environment where individuals feel motivated to contribute their best and support each other's success.

8

CONSTRUCTIVE CONFLICT: BUILDING STRENGTH THROUGH DIFFERENCES

'In the middle of difficulty lies opportunity.'

— ALBERT EINSTEIN

Trust within a team paves the way for open, passionate discussions on crucial issues and decisions vital for success. This trust empowers team members to openly disagree, challenge and question each other in pursuit of the best solutions, uncover truths and make exceptional decisions.

Conflict is a natural part of any team dynamic, yet the approach to conflict determines its impact. Constructive conflict, characterised by positive, solution-focused disagreements or differences of opinion, fosters team growth and improvement. Conversely, destructive conflict, marked by personal attacks and a reluctance to cooperate, can erode team unity and efficiency.

It is a misconception that all conflict is harmful. Conflict is often seen as a source of tension and a disruptor of peace. However, conflict can also be a force for good, driving innovation, enhancing problem-solving and refining decision-making processes. Aversion to conflict, a significant hurdle to team effectiveness, leads to superficial agreements that overlook vital issues and stifle diverse thinking.

CONSTRUCTIVE VS DESTRUCTIVE CONFLICT

Teams grounded in trust are fearless of challenging, questioning and disagreeing with one another – not for the sake of argument but to unearth the best solutions, uncover truths and make well-informed decisions. This concept leads us to the essence of constructive versus destructive conflict.

Constructive conflict is marked by a positive, solution-oriented approach to disagreements, leading to team growth and improvement. Differences in opinion are welcomed and seen as a crucial element for fostering creativity and critical thinking and ultimately driving the team towards success. On the flip side, destructive conflict, characterised by personal attacks, hostility and an unwillingness to collaborate, undermines team cohesion and productivity, eroding trust and stifling innovation. When I first mentioned conflict, which did you think of first?

To cultivate an environment where constructive conflict thrives, it's critical to distinguish between healthy, growth-inducing disagreements and the kind of conflict that damages team spirit and relationships. So, while the instinct to avoid conflict is understandable, recognising the potential for positive conflict can transform how we approach disagreements in the workplace.

Recognising that conflict is inevitable, and not inherently negative, is a pivotal shift in perspective for many teams. The fear of conflict, rooted in a desire to avoid tension and maintain a facade of harmony, can stifle important discussions and the expression of diverse viewpoints.

THE ROLE OF CONSTRUCTIVE CONFLICT IN TEAM DYNAMICS

Constructive conflict is a game-changer for team dynamics, focusing on the open exchange of differing viewpoints, ideas and opinions to achieve outcomes that benefit everyone involved. It can be the door opener for:

Better Decision-Making: Constructive conflict encourages team members to challenge assumptions, consider alternative viewpoints and critically evaluate solutions. This open, healthy debate ensures that decisions are well-rounded, thoroughly vetted and stronger because they incorporate a broad range of perspectives.

Innovation: It lays the groundwork for innovation and creativity by inviting the exploration of unconventional ideas and approaches. In an environment where everyone feels free to speak up and share their unique insights, creativity thrives. This openness can lead to groundbreaking solutions to complex problems and agile adaptation to new challenges.

Team Growth: Embracing these healthy exchanges fosters both personal and professional development. Respectful dialogue and active listening expand individual perspectives, improve communication skills and deepen understanding of colleagues' strengths and weaknesses. Navigating conflict together strengthens trust and cohesion and creates a supportive atmosphere where everyone feels recognised and appreciated.

Improved Relationships: Although it might seem counterintuitive, constructive conflict can enhance team relationships. Addressing disagreements openly and working together on solutions builds trust, empathy and mutual respect, forming the bedrock of strong, enduring relationships that can weather any storm.

Increased Engagement: When team members know their voices are heard, and their dissenting views are welcome, engagement and commitment to their work soar. Feeling empowered to express different opinions fosters a vibrant, dynamic team environment ripe for success.

As uncomfortable as it may seem, constructive conflict is the key to unlocking your team's full potential. Embracing and mastering constructive conflict propels teams toward unparalleled achievement and success.

COMFORT WITH CONFLICT

Engaging in productive conflict is important, but why do teams have so much trouble with conflict? In Chapter Seven, I highlighted that trust is the foundation of teamwork. Without trust, teams cannot, and probably should not, engage in unfiltered, productive, ideological conflict – trust needs to be established first.

But even after trust has been established, teams may still struggle with conflict. Individual viewpoints and comfort levels with conflict differ radically. Some people are comfortable screaming, shouting and arguing passionately; others hesitate to air the mildest of dissenting opinions because they don't want to offend anyone.

What about you? On a scale of one to ten, with ten being the most comfortable, how would you rate your own comfort level with conflict? And how about your team? How do they manage conflict?

Understanding conflict profiles is like unlocking a treasure trove of insights into team dynamics and individual behaviours. Like fingerprints, these profiles are inherent and deeply ingrained, shaped by our upbringing, cultural background and personal experiences. They dictate how we engage with conflict and influence our approach to communication and problem-solving.

In some cultures and families, conflict is viewed as taboo, leading to a preference for avoiding confrontation at all costs. In contrast, others embrace conflict as a natural part of interaction, engaging in passionate debates and reconciliations with equal fervour.

These contrasting conflict profiles manifest within teams, shaping the dynamics of meetings and interactions. Some teams operate in a harmonious environment where conflict is seldom seen. In contrast, others thrive on spirited debates and direct confrontations.

However, there is no one-size-fits-all approach to conflict within teams. What truly matters is whether individuals feel comfortable expressing their opinions openly and honestly. Great teams do not shy away from conflict; instead, they embrace it as an opportunity for growth and innovation.

By understanding and appreciating your team's diverse conflict profiles, you can establish a conflict culture that fosters open communication, mutual respect and collaborative problem-solving. This awareness empowers leaders to navigate conflicts effectively, leveraging each team member's strengths and fostering a culture of trust and accountability.

MITIGATING CONFLICT BEHAVIOURS THAT LEAD TO DYSFUNCTION

While embracing conflict can be beneficial for team growth and innovation, if left unchecked, it can also become toxic. Toxic conflict manifests in various forms, including personal attacks, aggression, passive-aggressive behaviour and an unwillingness to listen to opposing viewpoints.

Blame-shifting is a destructive behaviour where team members deflect responsibility onto others instead of taking ownership of their mistakes. Instead of collaborating to find solutions, they resort to pointing fingers, fostering an atmosphere of distrust and resentment. This avoidance of accountability leads to a lack of progress, unfinished tasks and missed deadlines, ultimately dampening team morale and productivity.

Ineffective communication exacerbates the problem, resulting in misunderstandings, information gaps and unnecessary conflicts. When team members fail to communicate clearly and openly, it fuels dysfunction within the team, hindering collaboration and impeding progress.

These behaviours can quickly spiral out of control, leading to dysfunction within the team and undermining trust and collaboration. Therefore, it's imperative that you remain vigilant and proactive in addressing these behaviours as soon as they arise. Set clear expectations for respectful communication and collaboration and intervene swiftly when toxic behaviours emerge, because if you fail to address toxic behaviours, chaos ensues. It's like watching a train derail in slow motion, with productivity plummeting and morale hitting rock bottom. Don't leave your team conflict unchecked.

Focus on having open and honest communication to quickly identify dysfunctional behaviour. Make sure teams have a safe space where everyone can freely share their thoughts, concerns and ideas without worrying about being judged or facing consequences. Regular team meetings, one-on-one check-ins, and feedback sessions can help encourage open communication and transparency within the team.

STRATEGIES FOR FOSTERING CONSTRUCTIVE CONFLICT

Constructive conflict is essential for igniting innovation and enhancing problem-solving within teams, and it begins with your commitment to nurturing an environment where open dialogue and respectful disagreement are welcomed and encouraged. So, how can you help your team achieve this?

Establish Psychological Safety: Cultivate a space where everyone feels comfortable sharing their thoughts without fear of criticism or backlash. This atmosphere of trust encourages everyone to freely contribute their unique perspectives.

Set Clear Expectations: Communication is key. Clarify how conflict should be managed within the team. Stressing respectful dialogue, the value of active listening and a solutions-focused approach can help ensure constructive conflicts.

Lead by Example: Your behaviour sets the team's benchmark. By showing openness to different ideas, admitting your vulnerabilities and demonstrating genuine respect for alternative viewpoints, you can inspire your teams to embrace constructive conflict.

Embrace Diversity: Valuing various perspectives and experiences enriches team discussions. Champion collaboration across varied backgrounds and skills, as this diversity often leads to breakthrough solutions.

Implement Structured Conflict Resolution Processes: Formal procedures for resolving conflicts ensure that issues are addressed systematically. This could mean setting aside specific times for open discussion or bringing in a neutral party to facilitate when necessary.

Encourage Active Listening: It's important for team members to truly listen to each other, ask questions for clarity, and strive to understand different points of view before reacting. Create strategies for individuals who talk over each other and allow sufficient time for people to speak and feel heard. This level of engagement can transform a potential conflict into a productive discussion.

Focus on Solutions: Steering conversations away from blame and towards actionable solutions encourages collaboration and prevents dwelling on the past. It's about moving forward and finding ways to overcome obstacles together.

Foster a Culture of Feedback: Create a feedback-rich environment. Provide regular opportunities for constructive criticism and suggestions to help the team view conflict as a stepping stone for growth and improvement.

Provide Training and Development: Offer resources and training on conflict resolution, effective communication and emotional intelligence to equip your team with the skills needed to engage in positive, constructive conflict.

For teams to thrive and innovate, you must intentionally foster constructive conflict. If you aren't comfortable with conflict, get help from an external consultant who can help you facilitate and create a feedback culture.

RESOLVING CONFLICTS COLLABORATIVELY

When you bring a group of diverse minds together, disagreements are inevitable. However, the true measure of a team's strength lies in how these disagreements are resolved. Embracing collaborative problem-solving turns the tide from competition to cooperation, fundamentally changing the team's trajectory towards collective success.

Active listening and empathy stand at the heart of resolving conflicts. They are two of the most important components of conflict resolution that can be achieved through joint efforts. Create a space where everyone feels seen and heard, where members can share their perspectives openly and listen deeply, without judgment. For instance, when a project team debates over deadlines, understanding each other's concerns, such as workload fears or resource constraints, through empathetic listening can pave the way to mutually acceptable solutions.

Identify shared goals: By focusing on what unites rather than divides team members – like a marketing team finding common ground in boosting brand visibility – they can creatively brainstorm strategies that serve the collective mission, not just individual agendas.

Consensus-building is about reaching agreement from all parties by considering their concerns and including their input in the decision-making process. This encourages individuals to take ownership and commit to the selected action. For instance, in a cross-functional team with differing opinions on implementing a new software system, consensus-building may require in-depth discussions to tackle usability, training and integration issues before reaching a conclusion.

HANDLING DIFFICULT CONVERSATIONS

Difficult conversations are inevitable in professional life, yet they often evoke discomfort and anxiety. Although they may seem daunting, they're crucial for growth. They enable you to address conflicts head-on, fostering understanding and resolution. Navigating these conversations with empathy and honesty can strengthen relationships, build trust and unearth solutions that benefit everyone involved. Avoiding them only prolongs the issue, leading to resentment and hindered progress.

Navigating tough conversations about performance issues and conflicts or providing constructive feedback is crucial for preserving positive dynamics and nurturing a conducive work atmosphere. Here's how to tread these waters with care:

Prepare and Plan: Reflect on your approach to a sensitive dialogue well in advance. Lay out the key points to address and clarify the conversation's purpose. Anticipate potential reactions or objections, envision the desired outcome and navigate the conversation confidently.

Choose the Right Time and Place: The success of a difficult conversation often hinges on timing and setting. Find a moment when both parties are calm and free from distractions, and select a private, neutral space for an open, uninterrupted dialogue. Initiating these conversations in tense or public settings can amplify stress and hinder clear communication.

Use Active Listening: Show empathy and understanding by actively listening. Let the other person share their thoughts and feelings without interruption, paying attention to what and how they say it. Validating their viewpoint fosters trust and openness, smoothing the path to resolution.

Be Clear and Specific: Clarity is key. Use concrete examples to illustrate your points and avoid ambiguity. Focus on actions or behaviours rather than making personal judgments. Honesty, respect and professionalism pave the way for constructive dialogue.

Remain Calm and Empathetic: Emotions might run high, but maintaining composure is essential. Keep a neutral tone, resist defensiveness or aggression and empathise with the other's perspective, even if there's disagreement. Acknowledging their feelings while seeking a solution helps keep the conversation productive.

Collaborate on Solutions: Foster a spirit of cooperation by jointly exploring solutions and brainstorming constructive approaches. Inviting the other party to partake in decision-making bolsters their investment in the outcome, enhancing the chances of a mutually agreeable resolution.

Follow-Up: Post-conversation, touch base to confirm understanding and reiterate the action plan. Showing appreciation for their openness and recommitting to the issue's resolution underlines the importance of the dialogue and aids in ensuring effective implementation.

Consider this scenario: a team finds itself entangled in friction due to conflicting communication styles among its members. Instead of allowing the tension to fester, a proactive leader convenes a meeting to address the underlying issues. In this meeting, the team is encouraged to openly express their concerns while others listen attentively, fostering an environment of trust and respect.

Through this open dialogue, the team identifies common ground and establishes communication norms that honour each member's preferences. The outcome? Enhanced cooperation, minimised miscommunication and fortified bonds among team members. By proactively addressing communication challenges, the team resolves conflicts and strengthens its collective effectiveness and cohesion.

GIVING FEEDBACK

Effectively delivering feedback in a constructive manner is a vital skill for leaders, yet it's often challenging due to feelings of stress, fear and guilt. Many of us avoid giving feedback altogether, opting for comfort over courage. However, failing to address issues can lead to unresolved conflicts, heightened tension and decreased team morale and engagement. The Three-Part Message was formulated to support people in developing assertiveness skills, but because it is simple and effective, I have used it to deliver feedback with great results.

The Three-Part Message

- **Separate the Person From the Problem:** Describe the behaviour or problem in a brief, factual and non-judgmental manner. Do not get personal or share your interpretations – describe what you have observed.
- **Communicate Your Feelings:** Describe how that problem or behaviour made you feel.
- **Describe the Wider Effect:** Describe the tangible consequences the problem or behaviour has on you or the team.

The Three-Part Conversation:

'**When you** (describe the problem / behaviour non-judgmentally), **I feel** (communicate your feelings) **because** (describe the effect on you).

Examples:

'When you are frequently late to our meetings, the rest of us feel disrespected because we waste our valuable time waiting for you.'

'When you don't verify your work before giving it to me, I feel frustrated because I end up staying later in the office correcting your mistakes and miss out on valuable time with my family.'

Think of two to three upcoming situations where it could be useful to apply this framework.

BRILLIANT TEAMS AND CONFLICT

When it comes to conflict, your brilliant team will:

- Ensure that the hard issues get discussed.
- Have difficult conversations professionally.
- Resolve conflicts promptly.
- Deal with conflict collaboratively because relationships matter.
- Voice opinions even if it makes others uncomfortable.

KEY TAKEAWAYS

- **Embrace Constructive Conflict**: Trust-based teams enable open, passionate dialogue on crucial matters, encouraging members to constructively challenge and question each other. This leads to better decisions, uncovering truths and achieving organisational success.
- **Distinguish Between Constructive and Destructive Conflict**: Constructive conflict fosters growth and innovation by encouraging diverse perspectives and solution-oriented discussions. In contrast, destructive conflict, marked by personal attacks and unwillingness to cooperate, erodes team cohesion and productivity.
- **Recognise the Value of Conflict**: Viewing conflict as inherently negative overlooks its potential benefits. Constructive conflict drives innovation, enhances problem-solving and refines decision-making, making it a vital component of effective team dynamics.
- **Foster an Environment for Constructive Conflict**: Creating a culture where team members feel safe to express differing opinions encourages collaboration and leverages collective intelligence, leading to remarkable outcomes.

- **Establish a Culture of Accountability**: Encouraging accountability among team members enhances the benefits of constructive conflict, leading to increased individual productivity and collective team cohesion.

9

COMMUNICATION: THE LIFELINE OF TEAM INTERACTION

'The most important thing in communication is hearing what isn't being said.'

— PETER F DRUCKER

Communication is the bridge that connects us with others. It's the basis of all human interaction, connecting individuals and facilitating the exchange of ideas, thoughts and emotions. It encompasses the tone we convey, words we choose, listening skills, energy we exude and non-verbal cues. Both conscious and unconscious, communication influences how others perceive and react to us. Even in moments of silence or absence, our actions – or lack thereof – speak volumes, showcasing that communication is constant, even when we're not actively speaking.

Think back to the last time you engaged in a truly effective conversation where both parties felt heard and understood, resulting in a meaningful exchange. These interactions require mindfulness and discernment, qualities that are often lacking, leading to unnecessary misunderstandings.

When communication breaks down, the consequences can be significant. We've all experienced it: messages misunderstood, emails misinterpreted and conversations lost in translation. Suddenly, deadlines are missed, projects veer off track and tensions simmer below the surface. Poor communication creates confusion, frustration and a lack of trust. It's like navigating a maze blindfolded – frustrating, inefficient and ultimately unproductive. Without clear and effective communication, tasks become tangled, expectations unclear and collaboration suffers.

Communication stands at the heart of our teams, making it the most crucial skill we possess in the workplace. It serves as the conduit through which we learn, inform, decide and share information with our teams, leaders, stakeholders and customers. Understanding the pivotal role of communication marks the initial stride towards enhancement.

We can mitigate misunderstandings and forge stronger connections by nurturing open dialogue, active listening and clarity in our interactions. Smooth communication paves the way for ideas to flourish, conflicts to be resolved and progress to march forward unhindered.

UNDERSTANDING THE BASICS OF COMMUNICATION

Effective and authentic communication is immensely important in both personal and professional realms. It serves as a basis for achieving supportive relationships, whether among friends or colleagues. In our increasingly digital society, where face-to-face interactions are fewer and communication channels are diverse, it's imperative to continuously adapt and refine our communication practices.

Just as the world evolves, so must our approach to communication. Effective communication is a skill that requires ongoing cultivation. Similar to exercising our muscles to improve our physical strength, developing communication skills across various mediums – from written communication in emails to face-to-face meetings – is essential.

Dedication to honing communication skills leads to greater alignment and impact in both personal and professional spheres. However, mastering communication requires patience, time and energy. It entails understanding how to convey conversations or messages effectively, considering factors like tone of voice, pacing and body language, which significantly influence the message's reception and interpretation.

Verbal communication breathes life into our ideas, whether expressed through casual conversations, structured meetings, or digital platforms. It's more than the words we choose; it's about the tone, pace, and volume that collectively convey the speaker's true intent. Body language, often louder than spoken words, adds depth to our communication. A smile or crossed arms can convey a myriad of emotions, reflecting the true sentiments behind our words. When verbal and non-verbal cues align, our message is clear and trustworthy. However, inconsistencies between them breed confusion and scepticism, sending mixed signals that undermine effective communication.

Clarity is paramount in written communication, such as emails or reports at work. Unlike verbal communication, we can't rely on tone of voice or facial expressions to convey meaning. This makes written communication powerful yet challenging; the words alone must effectively convey our intended message. Misinterpretations – like writing in capital letters being interpreted as someone shouting at you – highlight the importance of clear written communication. A well-crafted message ensures the recipient understands our meaning accurately.

Listening, often overlooked but crucial, plays a significant role in effective communication, particularly for leaders. Again, it is more than hearing words; it's about fully engaging, understanding and responding in a manner that fosters connection. Active listening acknowledges and values the speaker's perspective, fostering respect and creating an environment where individuals feel genuinely seen and heard. Good listening involves giving undivided attention, comprehending the message and responding appropriately. Assessing your listening skills can provide valuable insights into areas for improvement.

To communicate effectively, we need to ensure that our words, tone and body language all convey the same message, eliminating confusion. This also means being open to hearing others' ideas and views. When we do this right, it leads to better teamwork and everyone feeling understood and appreciated.

THE IMPORTANCE OF COMMUNICATION IN TEAMS

Effective communication enhances our professional lives, greatly influences our personal relationships and significantly influences team dynamics and overall performance. When communication is clear and consistent, teams operate more efficiently, resolve conflicts more swiftly, and cultivate a more positive work environment.

Research conducted by the Project Management Institute reveals that ineffective communication is the leading cause of project failure in one-third of cases and negatively affects project success in over half of instances.[1] Additionally, a survey conducted by Salesforce found that 86% of executives, employees and educators attribute failures in the workplace to ineffective communication.[2] These statistics highlight how important communication is in the success of teams and projects.

When team members communicate effectively, they can swiftly align their goals, collaborate more efficiently and navigate

---

1. Project Management Institute. May 2013. 'Pulse of the Profession' Report.
2. Salesforce. August 2014. How soft skills are crucial to your business.

challenges with greater agility. This can lead to stronger bonds and mutual understanding, and through clear, respectful communication, we can bridge cultural gaps, resolve conflicts and work together to achieve common goals.

Inspiring and empathic communication can foster the environment needed to increase motivation, accountability, job satisfaction and, ultimately, team performance. Investing in improving team communication is beneficial for project outcomes and crucial for your organisation's sustained growth and success.

ACTIVE LISTENING

To truly grasp another person's perspective, we must be fully present and receptive to listening. Although exceptional communicators are often said to excel at listening, very few people actually possess superb listening skills. Within teams, conversations frequently suffer from low levels of active listening, leading to missed opportunities for connection and learning. This deficit in listening proficiency prolongs decision-making processes, stifles potential synergy and leaves innovation unexplored.

The quality of our listening sends a clear message to those around us, whether we realise it or not. Our ability to listen influences how others perceive us within the company. When we listen attentively, we don't relinquish our stance or agree with the other person. Instead, we listen to gain insights, clarify perspectives and avoid making assumptions. This approach enables us to engage in more constructive conversations, exert influence and achieve optimal outcomes through mutually beneficial solutions. There are several ways we can approach listening:

Ignore – You make no effort, and you show it.

Pretend to Listen – You give the appearance of listening but are not.

Selective Listening – You listen to only what interests you.

Assumptive Listening – You rely on your assumptions of how the other person feels and what they will say next. This results in us finishing their sentence or interrupting.

Comparative Listening – You listen to the words and compare them with your own experience. You remain in your own bubble and aren't fully open to the other person's world.

Engaged Listening – You listen with the intention of fully understanding the speaker's situation, feelings and experience. You resist offering solutions, defending or explaining yourself and instead, sit in their world with them.

An increased awareness of the options available enables you to consciously choose relative to the person or topic and connect deeper in your conversations.

THE ROLE OF PERSONALITY DIFFERENCES IN COMMUNICATION

We've all experienced that moment in the workplace where someone just rubs us the wrong way. It could be an everyday irritant or someone who seems to target us specifically. Very few people wake up with the intent of making someone else's day miserable. Often, perceptions and frustrations arise from fundamental differences in our personalities.

Personality differences significantly affect how we communicate and interact with others. Each person has unique preferences, tendencies and ways of processing information, which directly impact their communication style. One widely recognised framework for comprehending these personality differences is the DiSC assessment, which categorises individuals into different personality types and communication preferences based on various dimensions. This makes it easier to understand the people around us.

For instance, introverted individuals may feel more comfortable communicating in writing than participating in group discussions. Extroverts, on the other hand, may thrive in social settings and prefer face-to-face interactions. Similarly, individuals with a preference for thinking may prioritise logical reasoning and factual information in their communication. In contrast, those with a preference for feeling may emphasise empathy and emotional connections.

Understanding these personality differences is essential for effective communication. It enables you to tailor your communication style to better resonate with those around you. For example, you may need to adapt your approach when communicating with team members of varying personality types to ensure your message is received and understood accurately.

Adapting our communication style isn't about being inauthentic but about respecting and valuing the other person's perspective. This powerful skill can lead to more effective interactions and stronger relationships within our teams. Different personality types can greatly impact how we express ourselves and interpret others' messages and how we are perceived.

Recognising and adapting to different personality types goes beyond simply improving communication; it's about appreciating the diverse ways in which we all process information and convey our thoughts. Through practices such as active listening, flexibility and respect, we can create an environment where each personality type feels acknowledged and respected.

By embracing these strategies and remaining mindful of personality differences, individuals can enhance mutual understanding, foster collaboration and cultivate stronger relationships in both personal and professional contexts. Effective communication helps us navigate the intricacies of human interaction and work towards shared objectives as a cohesive team.

If you would like to learn more about this subject or take your DISC assessment, please visit:

https://linktr.ee/bebrilliantconsultancy

ADAPTING YOUR COMMUNICATION STYLE

Adapting your communication style in the workplace is like having a Swiss Army knife in your pocket – it's versatile and incredibly handy. Not everyone responds the same way to a one-size-fits-all approach – some team members thrive on clear, direct instructions, while others prefer a more collaborative, open-ended dialogue.

The essence of effective leadership lies in your ability to tailor your communication to meet your team member's individual needs. This goes beyond altering your message; it involves understanding their preferences, meeting them where they are and adjusting your style to foster openness and trust. This level of flexibility strengthens interpersonal relationships and boosts team morale and overall effectiveness.

In the mosaic of today's workplace, with widening generational gaps, cultural diversity and varied personality types, being adaptable in your communication approach is imperative. Remember the power of adaptability, whether you're leading a team meeting, providing feedback or bridging differing viewpoints. It ensures everyone feels valued and heard, cultivating a cohesive and vibrant team environment.

Adjusting your communication style first requires self-awareness and understanding. Tools like the DiSC assessment can provide insights into your natural communication tendencies. But the real magic happens when you apply this knowledge, tweaking your approach based on the person you're engaging with and the context of your interaction.

Whether you're dealing with someone who appreciates directness or someone who values emotional connection, your ability to shift gears can significantly impact the effectiveness of your communication. It's about reading the room, tuning into non-verbal cues and crafting your message to resonate with the listener. By mastering the art of communication adaptability, you're not just talking; you're truly connecting, fostering an environment where every team member can thrive.

DIGITAL COMMUNICATION AND REMOTE TEAMS

Digital advancements have completely changed how we work together and communicate. Thanks to social media, virtual meetings and emails, teams can work together from anywhere in the world. This means people in different places can collaborate more easily and efficiently than ever before.

Despite digital communication's benefits, some particular challenges and considerations must be addressed. One common problem involves the potential for miscommunication and misunderstandings in digital interactions. Written communication can lack nonverbal cues and tone of voice, potentially leading to misunderstood or ambiguous messages, therefore, it is important to uphold clarity, conciseness and accuracy in digital communications to convey information and avoid misunderstandings effectively.

It's also crucial to remember our digital manners. This means replying to messages promptly, using professional language and respecting everyone's privacy. When working with people from different cultures, we must be mindful of their communication styles to ensure everyone feels included and respected.

Teams can explore different approaches and best practices to improve their digital communication, however, setting clear guidelines for digital communication is crucial to ensure that all team members are on the same page. This could involve defining expectations regarding email response times and adopting standardised message formats.

It is also essential to create a more respectful and collaborative atmosphere in virtual meetings. Encouraging active listening and empathy can significantly impact online interactions and enhance team dynamics.

Leverage technology to streamline communication. Project management and collaboration tools help teams stay organised and productive. They facilitate file sharing, task tracking and goal alignment, ensuring that everyone is working towards common objectives.

CASCADING INFORMATION

Cascading communication is like watering a garden – it ensures that vital information nourishes every part of the organisation, much like water reaching every plant in a garden. Essentially, it's about ensuring that crucial messages flow seamlessly through every level of the organisation.

Why is this level of communication so critical? Without consistent messaging, confusion can arise, and individuals may find themselves working at cross-purposes. Alignment is key; everyone should understand what's expected and be aware of developments throughout each team. Misunderstandings and misalignment can impede progress and make tasks more challenging.

A fundamental aspect of effective cascading communication involves determining who needs to be informed about what. Not every piece of information is relevant to every team member or department.

Therefore, it's essential to tailor the communication to ensure that individuals receive the pertinent details. How can we ensure that our cascading communication effectively reaches its intended recipients?

THE FIVE Ws

The Five Ws (Who, What, When, Where and Why) are a comprehensive framework for crafting your communication plan. Used alongside the RACI Matrix, they can help you clarify who's responsible for what and ensure the right people are informed and involved. To keep your communication effective, be mindful of:

Consistency: Keep your message the same at every level to avoid confusion.

Feedback Loops help quickly catch any confusion and reaffirm clarity, ensuring everyone understands. Consider how incorporating feedback could enhance the communication cascade.

Adapting the Message: Different groups might need the information presented differently, so consider how to adjust your message to make it clear to everyone.

Refine your approach to cascading communication, ensuring that every part of your organisation remains well-informed and aligned.

BRILLIANT TEAMS AND COMMUNICATION

When it comes to communication, your brilliant team will:

- Ensure all members feel heard.
- Effectively exchange views and opinions from all team members on important issues.
- Have a high level of open and honest communication across the whole team.

- Keep each other abreast of important issues affecting their areas of responsibility.
- Make time to celebrate successes and milestones.
- Make time for social interactions that build personal relationships.

KEY TAKEAWAYS

- **Understanding Communication Styles:** Recognise the different types of communication – verbal, non-verbal, and written – and their role in conveying messages effectively. Strive to be proficient in all forms of communication to ensure clarity and understanding within your teams.
- **Adapting to Personality Differences:** Acknowledge that individuals' personalities influence their unique communication styles. Use tools like the DISC assessment to identify these differences and tailor your communication approach accordingly. Embrace diversity in communication styles to foster better understanding and collaboration among team members.
- **Embracing Digital Communication Trends:** Embrace technology's impact on team communication, including emails, virtual meetings and social media platforms. Adopt effective digital communication practices and etiquette to maintain professionalism and clarity in online interactions. Encourage your team to leverage digital tools to streamline communication and enhance productivity.
- **Adapting Communication Styles:** Identify your communication style through self-assessment tools and be willing to adapt it according to different situations. Develop strategies for flexibly adjusting your communication approach to effectively convey your message and connect with team members on a deeper level.

EMOTIONAL INTELLIGENCE: HARNESSING EMOTION

'I've learned that people will forget what you said, forget what you did, but they will never forget how you made them feel.'

— MAYA ANGELOU

E motions are central to the human experience. Some experts claim we have over 400 emotional experiences every day! Emotions happen instantaneously before we have a chance to think logically about them. Emotional Intelligence (EI) is about understanding and learning to manage them.

Recognised as one of the top ten workplace skills by the World Economic Forum, EI plays a vital role in driving organisational change through leadership and company culture.[1] By enhancing empathy and compassion and fostering awareness and acceptance of emotions, EI empowers individuals to make a positive impact within their team.

EI, also called EQ (emotional quotient), significantly influences leadership and team performance. It encompasses the ability to

---

1. The World Economic Forum. October 2020. The Jobs Reset Summit.

perceive, comprehend, and regulate both our own emotions and those of others. Essentially, it involves navigating our inner landscape and mastering five key elements:

Self-Awareness: Knowing what you're feeling and why.

Self-Regulation: Being able to keep your emotions in check.

Internal Motivation: What drives you from the inside.

Empathy: Understanding what others are feeling.

Social Skills: How you interact and get along with others.

Glancing at these aspects, it's clear why EI is such a big deal in the workplace. People who can manage their emotions, stay driven and work well with others tend to stand out from the crowd.

Imagine a scenario where a leader possesses exceptional technical skills but lacks emotional intelligence (EI). The consequences can be chaotic. Picture a leader who lacks empathy, bulldozing through conversations without considering the emotions of their team members. Or envision an individual struggling to manage their emotions, reacting strongly to challenges and setbacks. The result? Dissatisfied team members, high turnover rates and a toxic work environment. Without emotional intelligence, communication breaks down, trust diminishes and morale plummets rapidly.

In every interaction, emotional exchanges occur, and emotions are contagious. This is why EI is so important when building and nurturing meaningful relationships. When we have a deeper understanding of ourselves and others, we can make more deliberate choices in our responses to situations. An emotionally intelligent individual is attuned to how others make them feel and incorporates this awareness into their interactions. They are also mindful of their own behaviour, ensuring they do not inadvertently upset or harm others.

Some people are more emotionally intelligent than others. However, none of us are 100% emotionally intelligent all the time; we can all be hijacked by certain triggers, situations, and/or people. The primitive part of our brain is wired to protect and keep us alive, so if a situation is deemed threatening, dangerous or unsafe, it results in emotional overwhelm that impedes rational thinking. This is when we react and behave in ways we may regret later.

With increased awareness of self and others, we can consciously pause, achieve mental clarity, change unwanted and disruptive emotional responses and manage ourselves and our relationships intelligently.

EI isn't about suppressing emotions or altering our inherent traits. Instead, it involves replacing less effective behaviours with more constructive ones and learning to harness our emotions in ways that benefit us and those around us. Developing EI is synonymous with personal growth. It enables us to make wiser decisions and cultivate deeper connections with others. It's a skill akin to a muscle we can strengthen over time.

The encouraging news is that EI is not fixed; it can be cultivated and enhanced. Those who prioritise the development of EI foster healthier relationships, inspire loyalty among their team members and adeptly navigate challenges. When assessing leadership abilities, it's important to recognise that while technical expertise is undoubtedly essential, EI is the guiding light in navigating complex and demanding situations.

THE IMPORTANCE OF EI IN TEAMS

EI holds diverse personalities together in a team, enabling effective collaboration, conflict resolution and collective problem-solving. Team members' levels of emotional intelligence will likely impact how well they can navigate emotional situations that will inevitably arise. Emotional intelligence is a vital consideration in the workplace for many reasons, but there are two that stick out:

- It is linked to higher job satisfaction for those with high EI/EQ and employees who work with or are managed by those with high EI/EQ.
- It is strongly associated with job performance.

EI AND JOB SATISFACTION

EI has long been recognised as a crucial factor influencing employee job satisfaction. Numerous studies have consistently shown that individuals with higher levels of EI tend to report higher levels of job satisfaction.[2]

Similarly, another study revealed that individuals with high EI, particularly those with high self-awareness, were less likely to experience burnout and more likely to report higher job satisfaction, especially in the public sector.[3]

However, it's worth noting that teams with lower emotional intelligence may exhibit negative behaviours such as cynicism, argumentativeness and fault-finding, particularly when under pressure. These tendencies can lead to challenges in providing constructive feedback and building trusting relationships within the team, ultimately impacting overall team performance and satisfaction.

---

2. Çekmecelioğlu, H. G., Günsel, A., & Ulutaş, T. (2012). Effects of emotional intelligence on job satisfaction: An empirical study on call centre employees. Procedia – Social and Behavioral Sciences, 58, 363-369. doi:10.1016/j.sbspro.2012.09.1012
3. Lee, H. J. 2017. How emotional intelligence relates to job satisfaction and burnout in public service jobs. International Review of Administrative Sciences [Advance Online Publication]. doi:10.1177/0020852316670489

EI AND TEAM PERFORMANCE

When EI is lacking, team dynamics and performance suffer. Communication becomes strained, trust erodes, and conflicts escalate. Leaders may struggle to inspire and motivate their teams, leading to disengagement and decreased productivity. Unchecked emotions often compromise decision-making, resulting in poor choices and missed opportunities. Teams lacking EI struggle to adapt to change, leading to resistance and decreased resilience. Without EI, the work environment becomes tense and toxic, stifling creativity and collaboration.

In contrast, high levels of EI in a team contribute to greater happiness and satisfaction in employees and better job performance. One study showed that EI significantly correlates with job performance, particularly recognising and managing the emotions of the self and others.[4]

THE IMPORTANCE OF EMOTIONAL INTELLIGENCE IN LEADERSHIP

Leaders with higher EI levels are great communicators. They listen attentively, express themselves clearly and carefully approach sensitive subjects. Their ability to understand the emotional context allows them to diffuse tensions effectively.

Emotional Intelligence is critical in leadership, offering the tools needed to recognise, comprehend and manage emotions within oneself and in others. This awareness aids leaders in handling complex situations calmly and empathetically, enhancing team dynamics and performance.

---

4. Tagoe, T., & E. N. Quarshie. 2017. The relationship between emotional intelligence and job satisfaction among nurses in Accra. Nursing Open, 4, 84–89. doi:10.1002/nop2.70

Such leaders lead with sincerity, authenticity, integrity and empathy. They create a positive workplace atmosphere that encourages trust, cooperation, and mutual respect by managing their emotions and leveraging their social skills. Teams guided by emotionally intelligent leaders are cohesive, resilient and capable of overcoming challenges to achieve exceptional outcomes.

Focusing on personal EI development, you can build healthier, more efficient work environments and establish stronger bonds with your teams, emphasising the indispensable role of emotional intelligence in your leadership. A leader who embodies and practices high EI can:

- Communicate their vision more effectively.
- Improve their persuasion and inspirational speaking abilities.
- Ensure appropriate responses to stressful and confusing situations at work.
- Manage their own emotions and the emotions of their employees (to an extent).

This leads directly (and indirectly) to a more efficient, effective and productive workplace.

THE EI MODEL

The EI model is a valuable tool for swiftly gauging one's level of emotional Intelligence. It provides a framework for assessing various aspects of emotional awareness and management. Self-awareness is the foundational step in this process, as it initiates conscious reflection and examination of one's own emotions. By understanding your own emotional responses and triggers, you lay the groundwork for understanding others more effectively. This self-awareness enables you to navigate interpersonal

interactions with greater insight and empathy, ultimately fostering
more meaningful and productive relationships.

	SELF	OTHERS
	Emotional Self-Awareness	Social Awareness
AWARENESS	What am I feeling? Why am I feeling this way? (Triggers)	What are they feeling? How can I better understand and value others? (Empathy)
	Emotional Self-Management	Relationship Management
ACTION	What do I want to feel? How can I manage my emotions so I can be effective? (Regulate)	How do I want them to feel? How do I create constructive and positive work relationships?

THE EI MODEL QUADRANTS:

Emotional Self-Awareness: The ability to recognise your
emotions and how they affect your thoughts, moods and
behaviour. Get a realistic understanding of your emotional
strengths and weaknesses and how they appear to those
around you.

Social Awareness: The ability to understand the emotions, needs
and concerns of others (empathy). It involves picking up on
emotional cues and recognising the interaction dynamics of others.

Emotional Self-Management: The ability to pause in order to
control or redirect impulsive or disruptive feelings or behaviours.
Achieving emotional balance and learning to manage emotions
healthily.

Relationship Management: The ability to develop and maintain healthy relationships. Lead effectively, communicate clearly, positively influence, collaborate and manage conflict.

To take an Emotional Intelligence assessment, visit:
https://linktr.ee/bebrilliantconsultancy

EXAMPLES OF EI AT WORK

Recognising high EI in the workplace is crucial for cultivating a positive and productive environment. But what exactly does it look like? Here are a few indicators:

Self-Awareness: Individuals with high EI are self-aware; they understand their own emotions, strengths and weaknesses. They can accurately assess their impact on others and recognise when their emotions influence their behaviour.

Responding to Upset Employees: This involves recognising an employee's moodiness, offering compassion and providing support. Those with low EI may ignore or criticise the other's feelings.

Behaviour in Meetings: Positive indicators of EI include listening attentively, allowing others to speak without interruption and maintaining focus on the meeting's agenda. In contrast, talking over others or contributing to disorganisation signifies lower EI.

Open Expression: High EI is shown by comfortably speaking and listening to others' opinions and emotions. Low EI is indicated by a reluctance to share feelings or intolerance towards differing views.

Handling Change: Workplaces with high EI navigate change effectively, embracing and implementing change initiatives, whereas those with low EI resist change and fail to support new directives.

Flexibility in the Workplace: High EI is evident when leaders recognise and accommodate employees' diverse needs, offering flexibility. Low EI is characterised by inflexibility and adherence to outdated practices.

Creativity and Innovation: Encouraging creativity and innovation signals high EI, as it recognises the value of employee input. Conversely, strict adherence to rules, with no room for creativity, suggests low EI.

Socialising Outside Work: High EI is often seen in workplaces where teammates engage in social activities, indicating strong bonds and relationship investment. A lack of social interaction outside work usually points to low EI.

STRATEGIES TO DEVELOP EI

Developing EI is a multifaceted process that involves self-awareness, empathy and the intelligent use of emotions. Here are some actionable steps for enhancing each aspect of EI:

Self-Awareness

Self-awareness is the foundation of emotional intelligence as it involves understanding your own emotions, strengths, weaknesses and behavioural patterns. To develop self-awareness:

- **Engage in regular self-reflection:** Set aside time each day or week to reflect on your thoughts, feelings and reactions to different situations. Journaling can be a powerful tool for gaining insights into your emotions and behaviours.
- **Seek feedback from others:** Actively solicit feedback from trusted colleagues, friends, or mentors about your interpersonal interactions and communication style. Use

this feedback to identify areas for growth and improvement.

- **Practice mindfulness:** Cultivate mindfulness through meditation, deep breathing, or body scanning. Mindfulness helps you develop present-moment awareness and enhances your ability to observe and regulate emotions.

Empathy

Empathy is the ability to understand and share the feelings of others. Developing empathy involves:

- **Active listening:** Practice active listening by giving your full attention to others when they speak. Focus on understanding their perspective without judgment or interruption. Paraphrase their statements to demonstrate that you are actively engaged in understanding their feelings.
- **Practice perspective-taking:** Make a conscious effort to imagine how others might feel in a given situation. Consider their background, experiences and emotions to better understand their perspective.
- **Show genuine interest:** Demonstrate empathy by expressing genuine concern for others' well-being and actively supporting them in times of need. Offer words of encouragement, validation or assistance to show that you care about their feelings and experiences.

Emotions

The intelligent use of emotions involves effectively managing and leveraging your emotions to achieve desired outcomes. To develop this aspect of EI:

- **Learn emotion regulation techniques:** Familiarise yourself with strategies for managing your emotions, such as deep breathing, progressive muscle relaxation, or cognitive reframing. Practice these techniques regularly to build emotional resilience and prevent emotional hijacking.
- **Develop conflict resolution skills:** Cultivate conflict resolution skills constructively by staying calm, listening empathetically to all parties involved and seeking mutually beneficial solutions. Practice active problem-solving and negotiation techniques to address conflicts collaboratively.
- **Foster positive communication habits:** Create a supportive and encouraging communicative environment by using assertive and respectful language, offering praise and recognition to others, and providing constructive feedback. Practice active listening and empathy in your interactions to build trust and rapport with your team members.

Remember that developing emotional intelligence is a lifelong journey that requires ongoing practice and self-reflection. By committing to continuous growth and learning, you can cultivate stronger relationships, make better decisions and thrive both personally and professionally.

Ultimately, EI plays a crucial role in successful leadership and team productivity. Leaders with high emotional intelligence are more capable of understanding, managing and connecting with their team members, enhancing collaboration, communication and productivity.

When improving your leadership abilities and creating a supportive team atmosphere, remember the importance of emotional intelligence in shaping your communication and choices. Keep focusing on developing your emotional intelligence. Engaging in daily reflection, practising empathy or attending training workshops can enhance your emotional intelligence to reach your leadership aspirations and foster a high-performing team.

BRILLIANT TEAMS AND EMOTIONAL INTELLIGENCE

When it comes to EI, your brilliant team will:

- Consistently display a high level of emotional intelligence.
- Assess social situations accurately by observing the interests, feelings and goals of others.
- Demonstrate empathy towards each other.
- Have a high level of self-awareness.
- Use their emotions intelligently to get the best out of others.

KEY TAKEAWAYS

- **Emotional intelligence is vital for successful leadership** and team performance, focusing on understanding, managing and using one's own emotions and those of others effectively.
- **EI encompasses five main elements**: self-awareness, self-regulation, internal motivation, empathy and social skills, all crucial for enhancing workplace dynamics and individual job satisfaction.
- **High EI leads to improved communication**, reduced conflicts and increased collaboration within teams by

fostering an environment of trust, respect and understanding.

- **Emotional intelligence is not innate** but can be developed through self-reflection, empathy practice and effective emotion management strategies. It contributes to personal growth and better decision-making.

- **Leaders with high EI inspire loyalty**, gracefully navigate challenges and cultivate positive work cultures that drive team success. This highlights EI's importance in effective leadership and team cohesion.

11

UNLEASHING THE POWER OF TEAM COLLABORATION

'If everyone is moving forward together, then success takes care of itself.'

— HENRY FORD

Why do some teams excel in collaboration while others struggle to make progress? The answer lies beyond mere enthusiasm for communication. It's about cultivating a blend of skills and behaviours and a shared dedication to achieving common goals.

Consider the essence of teamwork: it's about amalgamating diverse perspectives, talents and skills towards a unified objective. However, what truly distinguishes successful collaboration? It's the capacity to adapt, innovate and achieve remarkable feats in today's dynamic and interconnected landscape.

Effective teamwork drives organisational success. It merges various viewpoints, abilities and skills to pursue shared objectives and foster collective accomplishments. Successful collaboration is indispensable for teams to navigate change, generate novel ideas and attain exceptional outcomes in today's workplace. Embracing effective collaboration involves recognising the true purpose of joining forces. Is the goal crystal clear? Remember, disciplined collaboration is the linchpin; it's not merely about coexistence but about working together cohesively to deliver meaningful results. By nurturing a collective mindset and acknowledging shared victories, teams can cultivate a culture of collaboration, mutual support and collective responsibility.

WHEN COLLABORATION FAILS

Even the most extensive and disparate teams can collaborate effectively under the right conditions. While size, diversity and high levels of specialisation are increasingly crucial for tackling complex projects, paradoxically, these characteristics can impede a team's efficiency. The elements critical for a team's success can sometimes become stumbling blocks. Collaboration breaks down when team members focus solely on personal gains or agendas, and poor collaboration can be more detrimental than no collaboration at all.

Without strong leadership and support, team members are less inclined to freely exchange knowledge, learn from one another, adjust workloads to address unforeseen challenges, help each other meet deadlines or share resources. This hesitancy undermines the collaborative spirit, reducing the likelihood of team members feeling united in their success or failure, supporting each other's success or perceiving their goals as aligned.

According to Harvard Business Review, a team's natural inclination to collaborate decreases as it grows beyond twenty individuals.[1] Virtual collaboration poses significant challenges, with cooperation declining as teams become more dispersed –

---

1. Harvard Business Review. November 2007. Eight ways to build collaborative teams.

unless your organisation intentionally fosters a culture of virtual collaboration.

Diversity brings both benefits and challenges to teams. While diverse teams can offer a range of perspectives and ideas, they can also face barriers to collaboration due to perceived differences among members. These differences may include nationality, age, education and organisational tenure. Increased diversity within a team can lead to members working with individuals they may not know well or have never met before, potentially from different departments or even external entities. The greater the diversity and unfamiliarity among team members, the less likely they may engage in collaborative behaviours.

Additionally, the education level and expertise present within the team can impact collaboration. Teams with a higher proportion of experts may experience more frequent conflicts or obstacles to productivity.

THE IMPACT OF POOR COLLABORATION

When teams struggle to collaborate effectively, the repercussions are swift and profound. Research shows that miscommunication and duplicated efforts lead to a notable 20-30% drop in productivity.[2] This inefficiency arises from a lack of cohesion, resulting in tasks being needlessly repeated and important information slipping through the cracks.

The consequences of inadequate collaboration extend beyond productivity; it deeply affects team dynamics. Morale takes a significant blow, declining by 15-25%, as team members grapple with feelings of isolation and unappreciation. This decline in team spirit dampens enthusiasm. It contributes to a higher turnover rate

---

2. McKinsey. April 2023. The state of organisations 2023 Report.

as employees seek environments where they feel more connected and valued.

Furthermore, organisations with low levels of teamwork often experience a 50% reduction in innovation output. This decrease hampers the flow of fresh ideas, stalls new product developments and stifles improvements to existing offerings. Ineffective collaboration also leads to prolonged project timelines, with non-collaborative teams witnessing a 40% increase in the time-to-market for new products or services.[3]

These delays can be attributed to operational inefficiencies and a fragmented knowledge-sharing approach. Similarly, error rates in work output surge by 25-30%, highlighting the crucial role of collaboration in facilitating peer review processes and leveraging collective expertise to minimise mistakes.[4]

Customers experience the brunt of inadequate teamwork. When teams operate in silos, responsiveness to customer feedback decreases by 20%, leading to lower customer satisfaction and retention rates.[5] This disconnect from the customer base can have lasting consequences on an organisation's reputation and its ability to sustain and expand its market presence.

So, how can executives strengthen an organisation's ability to perform complex collaborative tasks, maximise the effectiveness of large, diverse teams and minimise the disadvantages posed by their structure and composition?

3. B A Barker Scott. 2024. Designing the Collaborative Organisation: A framework for how collaborative work, relationships and behaviours generate collaborative capacity.
4. Z Wang. Jan2020. Error rates of human reviewers during abstract screening in systematic reviews.
5. Shiftbase. March 2024. Working in silos: A business trap and how to escape it.

THE ROLE OF THE EXECUTIVE TEAM

It Starts at the Top

At its core, a team's ability to collaborate effectively reflects the ethos established by the organisation's top leaders. The success of collaborative endeavours within a team mirrors the commitment of senior executives to fostering social connections, demonstrating teamwork through their own actions and cultivating a culture where interactions among leaders and peers are seen as valuable gifts.

The conduct of senior executives establishes the precedent for collaboration across the entire organisation, even in companies with extensive staff. The seamless exchange of roles and responsibilities among members of the general management committee can signify a culture of mutual support and a comprehensive understanding of the business.

In the most collaborative organisations, executives strive to possess a deep knowledge and understanding of the entire business. This enables them to seamlessly assist each other with various tasks, such as leading a regional celebration, representing the company at a crucial external event or initiating an internal dialogue with employees.

Cultivating a 'Gift Culture'

A pivotal element of executive leadership involves integrating mentoring and coaching into daily practices, reshaping the organisational culture to view cooperation as a gift rather than a transaction. An effective method of informal mentoring is to guide new employees in building their networks right from their first day, emphasising the significance of personal connections in nurturing a collaborative atmosphere.

Fostering Community Spirit

While community spirit may emerge organically, strategic HR initiatives can significantly enhance it, promoting a sense of belonging through HR-sponsored events and activities. Supporting informal communities can play a central role in building a cohesive culture and laying the groundwork for ongoing collaborative success. For example, these communities could consist of a running club, cooking club or women's groups.

Executive leaders have a multifaceted role in cultivating a collaborative ethos, from investing in relationships and modelling teamwork to nurturing a culture of generosity and community. When an organisation models collaboration from the top, it can unlock the full potential of its teams and enable innovation, productivity and a shared culture of togetherness.

THE ROLE OF THE LEADER

Select the Right Leaders

Leaders play a crucial role in fostering high levels of collaborative behaviour within teams. However, achieving this requires flexibility in leadership style and approach. There has been ongoing debate about the most effective leadership style for leading teams. Some advocate for relationship-oriented leadership, emphasising the importance of trust and goodwill in facilitating knowledge sharing among team members. Others argue for task-oriented leadership, which focuses on clarifying objectives, ensuring a shared understanding of tasks and providing monitoring and feedback.

The most productive and innovative teams are often led by individuals who seamlessly blend both task and relationship-oriented leadership styles. These leaders are adept at adapting their approach based on the situation's specific needs and the desired outcomes. In the initial stages of a project, they demonstrate a task-oriented leadership approach. This involves:

- Clearly defining the goals.
- Engaging in discussions to ensure commitment from team members.
- Outlining the responsibilities of each team member.

As the project progresses, team members become more familiar with their goals and responsibilities, and initial tensions subside, these leaders transition to a relationship-oriented leadership style. They prioritise building rapport and fostering a collaborative environment where team members feel comfortable sharing knowledge and ideas. This shift allows for greater cohesion and synergy within the team as they work towards achieving their objectives.

TEAM FORMATION AND STRUCTURE

Given the importance of trust to successful collaboration, forming teams with previous relationships increases the chances of a project's success. Research shows that new teams, particularly those with a high proportion of members who were strangers at the time of formation, find it more difficult to collaborate than those with established relationships.

Newly formed teams must invest significant time and effort in building trusting relationships. However, when some team members already know and trust one another, they significantly reduce the time needed to build trust, can quickly hold each other accountable, and navigate the diverse perspectives on the team. Harvard Business Review, November 2007, reports that when 20% to 40% of the team members are already well connected, the team has stronger collaboration right from the start.

DEVELOP COLLABORATIVE SKILLS

Consider that some of your teams may have the desire to cooperate but lack the necessary skills to effectively work together. It's essential to develop specific collaborative skills that are crucial for fostering synergy and achieving success as a team. These skills include various aspects, including appreciating others, engaging in purposeful conversations, enhancing emotional intelligence, improving communication, and effectively navigating and resolving conflicts in a manner that fosters creativity and adds value.

Investing in targeted training programs is vital to address this gap and enhance your team's collaborative capabilities. For instance, training in appreciating others helps team members recognise and value each individual's unique contributions to the team and can cultivate a culture of respect, mutual admiration and collaboration.

Similarly, mastering the skill of engaging in purposeful conversations ensures that team conversations are not merely exchanging information but are driven by a clear intent and direction, aligning individual efforts with the team's overarching goals.

Providing your team with tools and strategies to creatively and productively resolve conflicts can turn potential obstacles into opportunities for innovation and growth, strengthening the team's resilience and fostering a more cohesive and productive working environment.

UNDERSTANDING ROLE CLARITY AND TASK AMBIGUITY

What fosters collaboration more effectively, a meticulously outlined roadmap towards the objective or clear definitions of each team member's role? Contrary to popular belief, clarity regarding individual roles significantly enhances teamwork. When each team member fully understands their responsibilities, they can concentrate on their contributions without the distraction of role ambiguity or potential conflicts arising from overlapping responsibilities.

However, this does not diminish the importance of maintaining some level of ambiguity surrounding the task itself. Combining clear roles with a less defined path stimulates collaboration, particularly in projects requiring creativity. When the approach to achieving a goal is open to interpretation, team members are encouraged to offer their unique perspectives, fostering a dynamic exchange of ideas and collective brainstorming. This not only enhances team engagement but also drives the team towards innovative solutions and creative breakthroughs.

Cultivating a culture where roles are precisely delineated while the journey towards the goal retains an element of exploration is key to unlocking collaborative efforts.

Dismantle Silos

Silo mentality refers to the tendency within an organisation for different departments or teams to operate in isolation. This mindset can severely hinder efficiency and innovation by impeding the exchange of information and ideas across teams. It often fosters a culture of mistrust, diminishes morale and prioritises individual or departmental goals over the organisation's broader objectives. Sadly, it is a common occurrence in many organisations and the larger the organisation, the more silos form.

When individuals are entrenched in silo thinking, they overlook opportunities for collaboration and fail to recognise how different parts of the business can synergise effectively. Additionally, when people feel isolated or prioritise their needs over team objectives, it can lead to internal conflicts, power struggles and frustration among team members and across departments.

The key to dismantling silos lies in setting collaborative goals, insisting on open communication, encouraging the exchange of ideas and nurturing mutual support among team members. Implementing cross-department projects, job shadowing and regular cross-functional team-building events can bridge the gaps between different departments, promoting a deeper understanding and appreciation of each other's roles and contributions.

Prioritise maintaining clear and open lines of communication to ensure smooth information flow across the company. Hold regular team and all-company meetings and use digital real-time communication platforms to facilitate communication, share information, and foster collaboration. This will help you break down barriers and promote a trusting and open atmosphere.

Promote Knowledge Sharing

The knowledge exchange between teams can yield numerous benefits that significantly impact performance and drive innovation. Knowledge sharing catalyses innovation by fostering diverse perspectives and alternative problem-solving approaches among team members. When individuals contribute their unique insights and experiences, it cultivates a culture of creativity and continuous improvement within the organisation.

When team members freely share their knowledge and best practices, challenges are identified and resolved more quickly. Instead of duplicating efforts or working in isolation, teams can harness collective intelligence to address issues more effectively and efficiently. This accelerated progress is achieved by minimising the time spent on redundant tasks or rectifying oversights in insights. As a result, teams can allocate their efforts more efficiently, directing them towards advancing and achieving their goals with greater speed and precision.

To promote and facilitate knowledge sharing, teams can implement various strategies. One approach is to establish a centralised repository for storing and accessing knowledge. Collaborative tools, intranet platforms and knowledge management software can streamline the sharing of documents, insights and lessons learned among teams and across departments. These platforms provide a structured framework for capturing, organising and disseminating valuable information, fostering a culture of collaboration and continuous learning throughout the organisation.

Create incentives for sharing knowledge and ideas. Identify and appropriately reward team members who participate in knowledge-sharing initiatives and reinforce the value of sharing as part of your culture. Instilling trust within the team will motivate members to communicate and share more freely.

Strengthening your team's capacity for collaboration demands a strategic blend of long-term investments and tactical short-term decisions regarding team formation, role definition and task articulation. What worked effectively for simple teams in the past, composed of individuals who were familiar with each other and in close proximity, may not yield success in today's more intricate team dynamics.

Many of the barriers to collaboration witnessed today would have posed challenges regardless of the historical context. Whether in the past or present, teams require an optimal mix of team members, diversity, cross-border cooperation and specialised expertise to tackle the multifaceted challenges of today's global business landscape.

Consequently, it's imperative to recalibrate team models to align with the evolving demands of the contemporary business

184 BRILLIANT TEAMS

environment. By meticulously addressing the factors mentioned above, leaders can curate teams equipped with the breadth of expertise necessary to navigate complex business issues effectively, all while mitigating the potential for detrimental behaviours that may arise in the process.

BRILLIANT TEAMS AND COLLABORATION

When it comes to collaboration, your brilliant team will:

- Effectively collaborate across their respective portfolios.
- Believe that team success is more important than individual success.
- Regularly share experiences and knowledge that benefit the whole team.
- Actively avoid the creation of 'silos'.
- Go out of their way to help each other succeed.

KEY TAKEAWAYS

- **Develop a culture of openness and trust**: Encourage transparent communication and create an environment where team members feel comfortable sharing ideas and feedback.
- **Implement collaboration tools:** Invest in technology platforms facilitating easy information exchange and project collaboration.
- **Promote cross-functional projects:** Encourage team members from different departments to work together on projects to break down silos and promote understanding between different roles.
- **Provide training and development:** Offer training programs to enhance collaboration skills, such as active listening, conflict resolution and empathy.

- **Lead by example:** Demonstrate collaborative behaviours by actively participating in team discussions, seeking input from others and valuing diverse perspectives.

12

RESILIENCE: SUSTAINING BRILLIANCE UNDER PRESSURE

'Courage doesn't always roar. Sometimes courage is the quiet voice at the end of the day saying, "I will try again tomorrow".'

— MARY ANNE RADMACHER

When we speak of resilience, we often consider it the ability to bounce back from setbacks or challenges. However, resilience takes on a broader dimension in a team setting. It is the collective capacity of a team to endure stress, adapt to change, and emerge stronger from the adversities faced – a shared tenacity and commitment to move forward, regardless of the obstacles.

Brilliant teams are characterised by their ability to navigate through uncertainty, maintain focus amidst chaos and use challenges as catalysts for growth. Resilience in a team is like having a sturdy ship in the stormy seas of business. It is the capacity to recover from setbacks, adjust to change and persist in pursuing your goals despite challenges. Devoid of it, a company would resemble a ship without a rudder – drifting and susceptible to every wave it encounters.

Resilience isn't just about recovery; it's a key ingredient for sustained high performance. Research shows that, over time, team resilience is a strong predictor of increased performance. As ongoing global crises and rapid technological shifts continue to change how we do business, the ability to adapt quickly will only become more critical. Resilience is necessary for our work relationships to thrive in difficulties, otherwise it can lead to decreased engagement and productivity.

WHY ARE RESILIENT TEAMS IMPORTANT?

Our workplaces are the epicentre of constant change. From navigating the impacts of the COVID-19 pandemic to addressing geopolitical tensions and embracing technological advancements, the pace of transformation knows no bounds. This relentless upheaval extends beyond boardrooms and team meetings, permeating every facet of our lives. As a result, each of us is called upon to embody a new level of resilience, adapting to these dynamic shifts with unwavering determination.

Within this context, the impact on business is significant. Resilience has been shown to positively affect wellbeing, task performance and work engagement.[1] Resilient teams bounce back faster from challenges, adapt to new ways of working to increase efficiency and maintain a strong sense of cooperation amid change.

THE CHARACTERISTICS OF RESILIENT TEAMS

Within resilience teams, several distinct qualities shine through:

Team confidence is not a collection of individual egos but a shared belief in the team's capability to navigate challenges. This confidence is nurtured through clear goals, participatory decision-

---

1. A. Hartwig et al. April 2020. Workplace team resilience: A systematic review and conceptual development.

making, recognition of successes and supportive feedback in times of struggle.

Open dialogue and honesty underpin the team's ability to confront and resolve challenges together, ensuring that truth guides their collective problem-solving efforts.

Resourcefulness emerges as teams face adversity, with creativity, not resignation, pooling their collective intellect to forge innovative solutions and remain outcome-focused despite external pressures.

Compassion and empathy, where team members share triumphs and failures and genuinely care for one another, are complemented by humility and an openness to seeking and accepting help within the team, strengthening the collective resolve to tackle obstacles.

Humility: Can your team ask for and accept help from other team members? Resilient teams are willing to admit when a problem has become intractable and ask for help from other team members or the organisation. They do not hide their struggles but embrace the group's responsibility for facing challenges and finding solutions.

Clarity of purpose. Does your team have a strong sense of direction and purpose grounded in its values and principles? This clarity provides a guiding framework, helping it stay focused and motivated even in challenging times. By aligning its actions with its values, it can navigate obstacles with resilience and determination.

Ability to improvise and adapt to changing circumstances. Resilient individuals and organisations find creative solutions when faced with limitations or constraints, making the most of the available resources. This adaptive mindset enables them to overcome challenges and achieve their objectives without external support or intervention.

Developing resilience within a team demands a keen understanding of its members' individual capacities and challenges, particularly in areas like self-awareness and empathy that may not naturally be inherent to everyone. Begin by thoroughly assessing your team's current state and pinpointing areas of weakness or deficiency. Armed with this insight, you can craft targeted strategies to dismantle barriers and foster the pillars of trust, transparency, and self-awareness.

As a trait, resilience encompasses a spectrum of qualities, including acceptance of reality, clarity of purpose and adaptability to change. However, even with an understanding of these core attributes, the question remains: what steps should be taken if your team grapples with a resilience deficit?

STRATEGIES TO PROMOTE RESILIENCE

Challenges are inevitable. However, the onset of the pandemic in 2020 caught some organisations off guard, revealing a lack of essential skills within their teams. This realisation has left many business leaders pondering their next steps in cultivating resilience. Building teams equipped with the skills and resilience to weather uncertainty and change is paramount for companies to navigate turbulent times with agility while sustaining productivity and engagement. But how can leaders harness the concept of resilience to cultivate teams that are not only more engaged but also more effective?

Create Psychological Safety: This is vital to creating resilient teams. When an elephant is in the room, create 'honesty breaks' to encourage team members to share their thoughts and feelings. Any team member can call one and, if necessary, break into smaller groups (using breakout rooms if the meeting is virtual) to further encourage frank discussion.

Independent Observers: To help team members embrace frank assessments of their work, resilient leaders invite outside experts to offer an objective perspective on issues/team dynamics.

Story Sharing: To foster participation, trust and engagement, encourage team members to map out their life's journey, including highs and lows, and share highlights with the rest of the team. In being vulnerable, the team creates an environment where compassion and humility are welcomed.

Owning Challenges: Resilient teams express their fears and concerns with each other. To build trust and honesty, facilitate this process by encouraging people to admit fears or relationship challenges and canvassing the team for solutions. For example, a facilitator can ask each team member to express their feelings about the team's state and what problems exist. The facilitator should encourage team members to 'own' their part in any existing problems and not resort to blaming other teammates.

Show That You Care: Regularly demonstrate your interest in the team's progress by asking probing questions to understand underlying issues. Remember, asking is only half the equation; you must also listen carefully to their answers.

Temperature Checks: At the beginning of every meeting, ask everyone to rate their energy levels on a scale of one (low) to five (high). This simple and fast exercise will quickly determine whether someone needs attention or is outside their normal range of fatigue and frustration.

Commit to Building Each Other's Resilience: I call this 'co-elevation.' Establishing clear and unambiguous expectations around team unity and peer-to-peer support is essential. Any hesitation or reluctance to help a struggling colleague indicates that deeper interventions may be needed.

Ultimately, team resilience is like a battery. It needs to be restored and recharged regularly. Teams that take measures to do that will be better equipped and, more importantly, willing to undertake any challenge throughout the pandemic and beyond.

WHAT SKILLS DO YOU NEED TO DEVELOP RESILIENT TEAMS?

Improving your resilience skills can also empower your team to become more resilient. Prioritising emotional intelligence, flexibility and innovative thinking can positively impact team dynamics. However, you may require further development and support to nurture and lead resiliently. Here are some key areas to focus on:

The Ability to Empathise: Even in a hybrid environment, the need to connect is still present. While many perceive empathy as an innate trait, it can be taught and developed. Developing personal relationships with team members and equipping yourself with tools to handle difficult situations and conversations is especially important.

Reduce Bias: A diverse and inclusive environment is important for day-to-day wellness. Though most companies have increased their focus on workplace bias, the new dynamics of hybrid and remote work risk introducing additional forms of discrimination, like denying development opportunities to employees who choose to work from home. It's essential to guard against this bias when building careers and working with your team.

Maintain a Sense of Humour: Though it may not always make the list of essential leadership skills, I strongly believe you must try to maintain a sense of humour through changes and challenges. Develop the skills to lighten tough conversations and prioritise moments of levity and fun in the workplace, which can help the team navigate difficult times with resilience and joy.

Maintain Composure: Staying calm helps with decision-making and problem-solving and creates a good atmosphere for the whole team. Displaying calm and poise in tough situations boosts confidence and encourages team members to do the same.

Cultivate a Positive Team Attitude: It can make a difference when dealing with challenges and boost team spirit and motivation. Find, acknowledge and celebrate every achievement, even the small ones! Team members feel great and get pumped when they see their hard work, even the little things, is appreciated.

PROMOTE A SELF-CARE CULTURE

Imagine a business team resembling a group of exhausted marathon runners stumbling toward the finish line. When leaders and teams neglect self-care, it's like running on empty – eventually, you hit a wall. Burnout becomes the unwelcome guest at the table when we forget to care for ourselves. Productivity dwindles, creativity stalls and motivation wanes. Team members feel drained, stressed and on the brink of collapse.

Meanwhile, the quality of work suffers as fatigue sets in. Mistakes become more frequent, deadlines slip through the cracks and morale takes a nosedive. It's a downward spiral that's tough to break free from.

Stress and burnout don't just affect people's health; they also hurt how well your organisation can work and get things done. U.K. businesses face an annual cost of more than £700 million due to employees missing work because of burnout.[2] Particularly alarming is the tech industry, where 82% of employees teeter on the edge of burnout, a condition not isolated to tech alone but also prevalent across healthcare, service, tourism and construction sectors.[3]

---

2. Spill. Jan 2024. The cost of burnout for employers.
3. Mercer. 2024 Global Talent Trends Report.

Remarkably, two-thirds of full-time employees admit to encountering burnout at some stage in their careers, with remote workers reporting even greater susceptibility, possibly due to the merging boundaries between professional and personal spaces.[4] It's been reported that 58% of professionals have concerns about disappointing their manager or team, and 31% feel anxiety due to unrealistic work targets. This epidemic underlines the critical need for a shift towards proactive self-care and well-being maintenance, not only as a personal responsibility but as a cultural norm within organisations.

You play a pivotal role in this transformation. You should embody self-care practices for your own benefit and as a beacon for your teams, reinforcing that well-being is paramount. This approach can combat the immediate effects of stress and burnout and strengthen teams' and organisations' overall resilience, preparing them to navigate the complexities of the modern work environment with vigour and determination.

It's important to feel comfortable saying no (and encouraging the team to do the same) when you're overwhelmed with requests and need to set boundaries. Continuously catering to colleagues' needs can lead to exhaustion and prevent you from maintaining a healthy work-life balance. Remember to prioritise your own well-being and be open to delegating tasks when necessary.

Self-care isn't selfish, it's essential. When you and your team prioritise rest, relaxation and rejuvenation, you recharge your batteries and return stronger. This boost in energy leads to increased productivity, enhanced creativity and elevated teamwork. Ensure that you and your team prioritise activities such as getting enough sleep, eating well, staying active, practising meditation or engaging in mindfulness exercises. Here are some

---

4. Gallup. July 2018. Employee Burnout. The five main causes.

effective ways I've observed organisations prioritise staff wellbeing:

Monthly Life-Admin Day: Implement a company-wide day off each month, allowing team members to address personal tasks and errands. This day can reduce stress by providing dedicated time to manage life outside of work, ensuring the team returns refreshed and focused.

Flexible Working Hours: Encourage flexible working hours or remote work options, allowing team members to design their schedules around personal needs and peak productivity times. By accommodating individual life circumstances, this flexibility can significantly reduce burnout.

Mandatory Break Times: Establish and enforce mandatory break times throughout the workday, including lunch breaks where work discussions are off-limits. Encouraging short, regular breaks can help prevent mental fatigue and promote rejuvenation.

Wellness Workshops and Resources: Offer workshops on stress management, mindfulness and healthy living and provide access to resources such as counselling services or meditation apps. Educating team members on self-care practices and providing tools for implementation can enhance personal well-being.

Physical Activity Encouragement: Promote physical health by sponsoring gym memberships, organising team sports days or setting up walking meetings. Physical activity is a powerful stress reliever and can improve mental health.

Setting Boundaries on Work Hours: Clearly define work hours and encourage team members to disconnect after hours, including limiting after-hours emails and calls. Respecting personal time can help maintain a healthy work-life balance.

Personal Development Days: Allow team members a certain number of days annually to pursue personal development activities unrelated to their work duties, such as attending a seminar or taking a course on a topic of interest. Providing a break from routine work can contribute to personal growth and prevent burnout.

Mindfulness and Relaxation Spaces: Create a dedicated relaxation space within the office where employees can take short breaks to practice mindfulness or simply unwind. A physical space devoted to relaxation can underscore the company's commitment to employee wellbeing.

Integrating these practices into your team's culture can foster an environment that values and promotes self-care. This will significantly reduce the risk of burnout and enhance overall team resilience and satisfaction.

ENCOURAGE GRATITUDE

As a leader, maintaining a positive outlook on life is crucial. Your team members look to you for guidance on navigating both challenges and opportunities. Demonstrating resilience and a sense of enjoyment amidst difficulties can inspire and motivate your team, fostering a more cohesive and resilient environment.

Encourage your team members to cultivate gratitude by acknowledging and appreciating each other's efforts and accomplishments. Ensure that everyone feels valued and motivated to express gratitude through various means, such as encouraging messages, handwritten notes or team-wide celebrations. Practising gratitude boosts team morale, fosters mutual respect and strengthens personal relationships.

Start Meetings with Gratitude Sharing: Begin team meetings with a round of gratitude sharing, where each member mentions one thing they're grateful for, whether work-related or personal. This can shift the team's mindset to a more positive and appreciative state from the start.

Gratitude Board or Journal: Create a shared gratitude board, physically in the office or digitally, where team members can post notes of thanks or appreciation for support, achievements or even the small things. Reviewing the board regularly can boost morale and remind everyone of the positive aspects of their work and relationships.

Peer Recognition Programs: Implement a peer recognition program where team members can nominate each other for 'gratitude awards' based on helpfulness, collaboration or going above and beyond. Recognition can be shared in team meetings or through internal newsletters.

Resilience helps teams weather storms, foster a positive team culture, enhance collaboration and drive overall success. By embracing positivity, celebrating small wins, fostering gratitude, leading by example, promoting open communication and providing support and encouragement, teams can cultivate a resilient mindset that empowers them to overcome obstacles and achieve their goals.

BRILLIANT TEAMS WITH RESILIENCE

When it comes to resilience, your brilliant team will:

- Avoid dysfunctional behaviour.
- Consistently bring a positive attitude to the team.
- Rarely make errors due to lack of composure.
- Recover quickly from setbacks.
- Take good care of themselves to avoid stress and burnout.

KEY TAKEAWAYS:

- **Clarity of Purpose and Values**: Resilient teams possess a clear sense of direction grounded in shared values and principles. This clarity is a compass during challenging times, helping teams maintain focus and motivation and align their actions towards common goals despite obstacles.
- **Adaptability and Creativity**: The hallmark of resilience is adapting to changing circumstances and finding creative solutions within constraints. Resilient teams excel in improvising and leveraging available resources to overcome challenges, viewing limitations as opportunities for growth and innovation.
- **Shared Tenacity**: Beyond individual perseverance, team resilience manifests as collective tenacity – a unified commitment to persist and advance regardless of the difficulties encountered. It's about moving forward together, turning adversities into catalysts for strengthening the team's resolve and capabilities.
- **Emotional Intelligence and Mutual Support**: Key qualities of resilient teams include emotional intelligence, empathy and a culture of mutual support. Team members openly share successes and failures and offer and seek help within the group.

CONCLUSION

On the journey to building brilliant teams, we've explored the intricate dynamics that transform a group of individuals into a cohesive, high-performing unit. Our goal wasn't just to identify the mechanisms driving efficiency or innovation but to delve deeper into the fabric constituting a team's soul: its people, purpose and resilience in the face of change.

At the heart of every brilliant team lies a clear, compelling vision – a sense of purpose that transcends individual aspirations and aligns with a broader mission. This vision acts as the north star, guiding teams through turbulent waters and anchoring them in their core values. In the relentless pursuit of excellence, it's easy to lose sight of why we do what we do. However, the 'why' fuels our passion, drives innovation and fosters a culture of trust and collaboration. As leaders, our role is not merely to direct but also to inspire and instil a sense of belonging and purpose that empowers our teams to achieve the extraordinary.

The journey towards brilliance is paved with challenges, obstacles and setbacks. In these moments, the true strength of a team is tested. Resilience, the ability to adapt and thrive in the face of adversity, emerges as a defining trait of brilliant teams. This resilience is cultivated through a culture of support, open communication and mutual respect. It's about embracing our vulnerabilities, learning from our failures and viewing every challenge as an opportunity for growth. In doing so, we create an environment where innovation flourishes and where each member feels valued and empowered to contribute their best.

Building brilliant teams is an art that demands empathy, patience and a deep understanding of the human spirit. It's about fostering a culture where diversity is celebrated, each voice is heard, and every team member feels genuinely cared for. This sense of community and belonging transforms a group of individuals into a cohesive unit with a shared vision and common goals. This collective spirit enables teams to navigate the complexities of our modern world with agility and grace.

As we've seen, teamwork dynamics extend beyond traditional workspace confines. The advent of remote and hybrid models has redefined how we collaborate, presenting new challenges and opening up a world of possibilities. Embracing these changes requires a shift in mindset, a willingness to experiment and a commitment to continuous learning. It's about leveraging technology to foster connection, maintaining a sense of presence despite physical distances and finding innovative ways to sustain engagement and productivity.

The role of leadership is more critical than ever. Leaders must be the architects of culture, champions of change and custodians of their teams' wellbeing. This role demands authenticity, courage and a profound sense of empathy. Leaders must lead by example, show vulnerability, celebrate successes and gracefully navigate failures. They must create spaces where open dialogue is encouraged, feedback is valued and every team member feels empowered to bring their whole self to work.

As we conclude this exploration, it's clear that the path to brilliance is not a destination but a journey – a continuous process of growth, learning and transformation. It's marked by moments of triumph and periods of struggle, but above all, it's enriched by the shared experiences and deep connections we forge along the way.

Building brilliant teams is about more than just achieving business objectives or reaching performance targets. It's about creating something larger than ourselves – a legacy of impact, innovation and human connection. It's about shaping a future where work is not just a means to an end but a platform for expressing our deepest values and aspirations.

As you step forward into this future, do so with a sense of purpose, a commitment to excellence and a deep appreciation for the journey ahead. Build brilliant teams that are not just resilient in the face of change but are catalysts for transformation – teams that inspire, innovate and lead with heart.

Your greatest asset in this journey is your humanity – the capacity to connect, empathise, and uplift those alongside you. Embrace this ethos of co-elevation as you confront challenges and embrace opportunities in your evolving world. Leave behind a legacy of excellence that extends beyond the confines of your team, making a meaningful imprint on your organisation and the world at large.

Thank you for joining me on this journey. May your path to building brilliant teams be filled with learning, growth and boundless possibilities. Here's to the journey ahead and the brilliance you and your team will create together. Best of luck!

YOUR MAP AHEAD

CLEARER VISION, STRATEGY AND GOALS: Clear KPIs, a clear business plan, a shared sense of purpose, clear direction and disciplined strategic reviews.

SET PRIORITIES: Be clear from the beginning, allocate time according to priorities, better manage competing priorities and have honest discussions on priorities.

MORE RESOURCES: Improve resource accessibility, align resources to business objectives, better resource planning and better sharing of resources.

PROCESS IMPROVEMENT: Streamline processes, standardise processes, continuous improvement, improve internal processes and improve consistency.

MORE ACCOUNTABILITY: Challenge each other constructively, correct poor behaviour, stronger KPI reviews, hold people responsible and challenge poor performers.

BETTER MEETINGS: Clearer agendas, improved punctuality, better attendance, less time wasted and regular meetings for catch-ups.

REGULAR MEETING RHYTHM: Regular business reviews, regular team meetings, a stronger planning process, separate operational from strategic reviews and more strategic discussions.

TEAM BUILDING: Understand each other, share your strengths and weaknesses, build self-awareness and understand each other's personality and work styles.

TACKLE THE DIFFICULT ISSUES: Include more health debate, challenge each other, discuss the hard issues and don't avoid conflict.

CELEBRATE SUCCESSES: Celebrate achievements, increase recognition and reward, recognise goal performance and celebrate wins and milestones.

REGULAR FEEDBACK: Continuous performance feedback, constructive feedback and feedback on how to do even better.

IMPROVE COMMUNICATIONS: Communicate openly and honestly, keep everyone updated, share the big picture, share information and communicate decisions.

MORE COLLABORATION: One team approach, no silos, less 'them' and more 'us', all on the same page, working together for one goal.

MORE SOCIAL OCCASIONS: Social events, more time together as friends, social activity and regular social occasions.

CLEARER ROLES AND RESPONSIBILITIES: Clarify exactly who does what, clearly define job descriptions, get people to take ownership and ensure that everyone understands each other's roles and responsibilities.

ADDITIONAL RESOURCES

Here are additional resources to deepen your understanding of team dynamics and enhance your leadership skills. It's a curated selection of support items, courses and assessments to aid you and your team to be brilliant. Here is where you can find all the resources: https://linktr.ee/bebrilliantconsultancy

ASSESSMENTS

The Brilliant Team Audit

This pivotal tool, designed to complement this book, offers a comprehensive audit of your team's brilliance. By evaluating key performance and cultural metrics, this assessment delivers insightful feedback on your team's current state and identifies areas for growth. Accessing this tool will empower leaders with actionable data to enhance team dynamics, drive engagement and elevate overall team performance toward brilliance.

DiSC Assessment

A powerful tool designed to enhance self-awareness and improve interpersonal relations within teams. By identifying and understanding your DiSC profile, you can gain insights into your preferred communication styles, behaviours and ways of working. This assessment facilitates better teamwork by helping individuals recognise and appreciate their colleagues' diverse communication styles and strengths. Implementing the DiSC framework within your team can lead to more effective interactions, reduced conflict and a more cohesive and collaborative working environment. It's an essential resource for anyone looking to foster a culture of understanding and productivity in their team.

Emotional Intelligence Assessment

An insightful tool that measures an individual's capacity to recognise, understand and manage their own emotions, as well as the emotions of others. This assessment provides invaluable insights into how emotional intelligence influences interactions, decision-making and leadership styles. Upon completion, participants receive a detailed report outlining their strengths and areas for growth, along with actionable strategies to enhance their emotional intelligence. This tool is essential for anyone looking to improve their professional relationships, leadership capabilities and personal resilience.

Marketing Leadership Audit

A comprehensive evaluation designed to identify gaps in customer focus, team capabilities, marketing processes, strategic leadership and operational excellence. By examining these crucial areas, the audit helps leaders pinpoint areas for improvement to accelerate revenue generation. Upon completion, you'll receive a detailed analysis and actionable recommendations tailored to enhance your marketing strategy's effectiveness. This audit is ideal for leaders aiming to refine their marketing efforts, boost team performance and achieve superior results in a competitive landscape.

COURSES & WORKSHOPS

Strategy Planning Workshop

A meticulously designed session aimed at aligning your team's vision, setting clear objectives, and crafting a roadmap to achieve your organisation's goals. This intensive one- or two-day workshop is the catalyst your team needs to transition from ambiguity to clarity, ensuring that every member is not only on the same page but also fully committed to the journey ahead. Participants emerge with a shared understanding of the strategic direction, a robust action plan tailored to meet both immediate and long-term objectives and enhanced collaboration skills that will drive efficiency and innovation. The workshop facilitates deep dives into your business's challenges and opportunities, leveraging collective expertise to identify and prioritise strategic initiatives. By investing in a Strategy Planning Workshop, you're not just planning for success; you're laying the foundation for a cohesive, dynamic team equipped to navigate complexities with confidence and agility. It's an essential step for any team looking to sharpen their focus, optimise performance and achieve remarkable results.

DiSC One-Day Workshop

A transformative experience designed to bring the insights of the DiSC Assessment to life in an engaging, interactive format. Participants will delve deep into their individual profiles, uncovering the nuances of their communication styles and behavioural tendencies. This workshop, led by expert facilitators, offers practical exercises, group discussions and personal reflection opportunities, empowering attendees to improve interpersonal relationships, enhance team dynamics and foster a more collaborative workplace. The outcome is a day of profound (fun) learning that equips individuals with the strategies needed for more effective communication and teamwork.

DiSC Audio Course

This immersive learning experience is designed to deepen your understanding of DiSC personality profiles and how they can enhance team dynamics. Through eight comprehensive audio modules, you'll explore the nuances of different DiSC styles, discover strategies for more effective communication, and learn how to leverage your team's diverse strengths. This course equips you with the knowledge to create a more cohesive, understanding and productive work environment. It is an invaluable resource for leaders and team members aiming to foster a culture of collaboration and respect.

Leading Remote Teams Course

The Remote Teams On-Demand Course is your essential guide to mastering the art of managing and thriving within a remote work environment. Tailored for leaders and teams navigating the complexities of remote collaboration, this course offers comprehensive insights and practical strategies to enhance communication, foster a strong team culture and boost productivity from anywhere in the world. Participants will learn how to overcome common remote work challenges, implement best practices for virtual team building and leverage technology to maintain seamless operations and connections. Whether you're a seasoned remote team leader or adapting to remote work for the first time, this course provides the tools and knowledge to create a thriving, engaged and high-performing team.

TOOLS & TEMPLATES

Strategic Planning Template

An invaluable resource for leaders looking to crystallise their team's vision and objectives. This carefully crafted template guides you through setting achievable goals, outlining clear strategies and identifying critical milestones. Utilising this template ensures a focused approach to planning, enabling teams to align their efforts with overarching business aims and drive sustainable growth. It's an essential tool for any leader aiming to navigate their team through the complexities of today's business landscape with clarity and precision.

Balanced Scorecard Template

This comprehensive framework is designed to help teams measure and improve performance across key business areas. By focusing on financial, customer, internal process and learning and growth perspectives, this template allows leaders to establish and track relevant metrics, ensuring that their strategic actions align with long-term objectives. Implementing this template empowers teams to maintain a holistic view of their progress. It fosters a culture of continuous improvement and accountability. It's a pivotal resource for any team committed to achieving excellence and maximising their impact.

RACI Matrix Template

An invaluable tool for clarifying roles and responsibilities within any project or process. It outlines who is Responsible, Accountable, Consulted and Informed for each task, ensuring transparency and efficiency in teamwork. By utilising this template, you can prevent overlaps and gaps in team activities, enhance communication and streamline decision-making processes. This methodical approach boosts project management effectiveness and strengthens team cohesion by setting clear expectations for all involved. It's essential for teams looking to enhance collaboration and achieve seamless execution of tasks.

Meeting Effectiveness Toolkit

This toolkit is designed to transform your team meetings from time-consuming to productive and engaging. It provides strategies and checklists to plan and execute focused, efficient, and result-oriented meetings. This toolkit helps you set clear objectives, ensure active participation and follow through on action items, drastically improving the quality and outcome of your team gatherings. Ideal for leaders seeking to maximise their team's time and foster a culture of accountability and progress, this resource is a game-changer for anyone looking to elevate the effectiveness of their meetings.

BIBLIOGRAPHY

State of the Global Workplace report, Gallup. 2022

Harvard Business Reviews. March 2022. 'How-employee-experience-impacts-your-bottom-line'

Hogan, R., Raskin, R., & Fazzini, D. (1990). The Dark Side of Charisma. In K. E. Clark & M. B. Clark (Eds.), Measures of Leadership (pp. 343–354). Leadership Library of America.

Hogan, R. 1994. Trouble at the Top: Causes and Consequences of Managerial Incompetence. Consulting Psychology Journal: Practice and Research, 46(1), 9–15. https://doi.org/10.1037/1061-4087.46.1.9

Kaiser, R. B., R. Hogan, & S. B. Craig. 2008. Leadership and the Fate of Organizations. American Psychologist, 63(2), 96–110. https://doi.org/10.1037/0003-066X.63.2.96

Harvard Business Review. February 2022. 'Does-your-team-have-an-accountability-problem'

McKinsey Report. Capturing the true value of industry four-point zero.

Gallup. December 2018. Fostering Creativity at Work: Do Your Managers Push or Crush Innovation?

Adobe. How a Global Pandemic and Cultural Movements are Impacting the Industry.

WorkHuman Report, 2019. International Employee Survey.

World Economic Forum. May 2023. Future of Jobs Report.

Bloomberg Job Skills Report. 2015.

Gallup. Dec 2018. Fostering creativity at work.

PwC. Thriving in an age of continuous reinvention.

Spill, Feb 2024. Seventy workplace stress statistics you need to know in 2024.

https://www.gallup.com/cliftonstrengths/en/254033/strengthsfinder

Doodle. State of Meetings Report, 2019.

Patrick Lencioni. The Five Dysfunctions of a Team.

Gallup. Employee Engagement vs. Employee Satisfaction and Organizational Culture.

Gallup, How to Tackle U.S. Employees' Stagnating Engagement.

Forbes, Does corporate culture drive financial performance?

McKinsey. March 2019. Organisational culture in mergers. Addressing the unseen forces.

Google. Project Aristotle Report.

Project Management Institute. May 2013. 'Pulse of the Profession' Report.

Salesforce. August 2014. How soft skills are crucial to your business.

The World Economic Forum, October 2020. The Jobs Reset Summit.

Çekmecelioğlu, H. G., Günsel, A., & Ulutaş, T. (2012). Effects of emotional intelligence on job satisfaction: An empirical study on call centre employees. Procedia – Social and Behavioral Sciences, 58, 363-369. doi:10.1016/j.sbspro.2012.09.1012

Lee, H. J. 2017. How emotional intelligence relates to job satisfaction and burnout in public service jobs. International Review of Administrative Sciences [Advance Online Publication]. doi:10.1177/0020852316670489

Tagoe, T., & E. N. Quarshie. 2017. The relationship between emotional intelligence and job satisfaction among nurses in Accra. Nursing Open, 4, 84–89. doi:10.1002/nop2.70

Harvard Business Review. November 2007. Eight ways to build collaborative teams.

McKinsey. April 2023. The state of organisations 2023 Report.

B A Barker Scott, 2024. Designing the Collaborative Organisation: A framework for how collaborative work, relationships and behaviours generate collaborative capacity.

Z Wang. Jan2020. Error rates of human reviewers during abstract screening in systematic reviews.

Shiftbase. March 2024. Working in silos: A business trap and how to escape it.

A. Hartwig et al. April 2020. Workplace team resilience: A systematic review and conceptual development.

Spill. Jan 2024. The cost of burnout for employers.

Mercer. 2024 Global Talent Trends Report.

Gallup. July 2018. Employee Burnout. The five main causes.

www.ingramcontent.com/pod-product-compliance
Lightning Source LLC
Chambersburg PA
CBHW050526190326
41458CB00045B/6724/J